Skinning Catfish in Mary's Kitchen

SKINNING CATFISH IN MARY'S KITCHEN
Tales of Hunting, Fishing, Trapping, and Life in the Woods

WILL BRANTLEY

Essex, Connecticut

An imprint of The Globe Pequot Publishing Group, Inc.
64 South Main St.
Essex, CT 06426
www.globepequot.com

Copyright © 2026 by Will Brantley

All rights reserved. No part of this book may be reproduced in any form or by any electronic or mechanical means, including information storage and retrieval systems, without written permission from the publisher, except by a reviewer who may quote passages in a review.

British Library Cataloguing in Publication Information available

Library of Congress Cataloging-in-Publication Data available
ISBN 9781493094455 (cloth) | ISBN 9781493095643 (epub)

To Mishkin.
Let's ramble on.

Contents

Foreword xi
Introduction xvii

Chapter 1: The Opener 1
   Shagbarks 3
   The Lesson of the Shattered Nipple 5
   Bullfrogs in Aunt Tammy's Sh*t Pond 7
   Lockjaw 9
   Trout Fishing with Kenny Dean 16
   Joe's Pheasant 20
   On BB Gun Safaris 26

Chapter 2: Young Bucks 29
   A Date with Some Deer Piss 31
   On Face Paint 35
   The Turkey Truants 36
   Old Trusty 41
   Skinning Catfish in Mary's Kitchen 45
   Snakes, Smallmouths, and a Four-Way Wrench 47
   Autumn in August 53
   Ode to the Boat-Paddle Ruger 55
   Paid to Fish 58
   Baker's Thumb 61
   With a Fish Fry at the End 63

Chapter 3: Birds, Lions, Flatheads, and Murder 67
   Out of the Smoke 69
   The Bird Hunter's Club 71
   Lil's Last Hunt 76
   Handfishing on the Yeah-Zoo River 79
   The Voodoo Box 91
   Bluewing Weather 93
   The Lion Hunters 96
   The Bluegill Date 105

Chapter 4: On Assignment 107
   King of the Swamp .109
   Mule Deer Are Easy .113
   Nora and the Moose .115
   Bo Whoop Comes Home 120
   Redemption Bull 125
   Tahr Camp 129
   First Sit 134
   The Tiniest Buck I Ever Hunted 137
   Fresh Beavers and Big Bears 141
   Elk Don't Gobble 145

Chapter 5: The Journey 151
   My New Creed 153
   The Craig's List Camper 154
   The Coyote Trapper .157
   A Limit with Wade .158
   Confessions of a Turkey Purist 163
   Dad's Call 167
   Little Lockjaw 170
   Larry's Legacy 172
   Lost and Found 176
   20 Summers of Blood Sport 180

Contents

Chapter 6: The Trip Home 185
   On Fly Fishing 187
   Hoola-Bear 188
   Beavercue 191
   Trout Bums 194
   Lake Locals 197
   On Gates 199
   Born-Again Duck Hunter 202
   Purpose Point 205
   The Thrash-Metal Turkey 208

Afterword and Acknowledgments 213

Foreword

I am a Yankee cat lover who drinks hazy IPAs. Will Brantley is a Kentuckian who drinks straight whiskey and whose Catahoula leopard dog would gladly snack on my furballs. I love fly fishing. Brantley loves to make fun of fly fishing, often while wrestling catfish with his bare hands. And yet it works somehow. I've been Brantley's editor and friend for more than 15 years. If we fundamentally agree on anything, it's that our friendship is built mainly on arguing over who is right and who is full of shit.

There was a time when I was always right. That is, I'm still always right, but there was a time when Brantley accepted it, no questions asked, no smartass backtalk. He was a newly married twenty-something trying to make a go at freelance writing, and I was 15 years in as an editor with *Field & Stream* (*F&S*). A colleague gave him my number, we chatted, and I assigned him two basic how-to stories on spec: one about the best spots to tag an early season buck and another on where to aim at a broadside pig. It was the summer of 2010 when he submitted those first two pieces. I read them—and couldn't believe my luck.

At the time, we *F&S* editors had been bemoaning the lack of young talent in the outdoor writing world, often wondering, *Where are the David E. Petzals and the Phil Bourjailys, the Eddie Nickenses, and Bill Heaveys of this generation?* And here, seemingly out of the blue, was this kid from western Kentucky who not only lived to hunt and fish and seemed to know his stuff but could also write about it with clarity and style.

That doesn't come along every day, so I gave him a pile of new how-to stories to write for *F&S*, and for a good long while, things went along just as they should: Brantley sent in stories, and I told him what was wrong with them. Then—and this seems hard to believe now—he fixed them without so much as a whimper.

But there was a problem. The more stories Brantley wrote, the less I could find wrong with them. In 2015, he became hunting editor of *F&S*, which is a pretty heady title. It meant that he'd be writing a regular column in addition to frequent feature stories. It meant that his name would routinely appear alongside many of his writing heroes. And it meant that he would be on much better footing to argue with me.

It was around this time that the two of us first hunted together out in western Nebraska for spring turkeys. I figured it would be a good opportunity to solidify the pecking order. So, let me tell you a little story about how that went.

We'd worked three gobblers at dawn on the first morning, but when they slipped past us with a pack of hens, we found ourselves playing catchup as the birds filtered away into a vast, rolling expanse, up one open hillside and down the next. It was a perfect spring morning on the prairie, a light breeze making waves in the grasses and carrying birdsong.

Taking it all in, I said, "I've got to tell you, Brantley, I could listen to those meadowlarks sing all day."

"That's great, Hurteau," he answered, marching to the top of a hill. "I could listen to you *not* talk about songbirds all day."

"They're not even true larks, you know? They're part of the blackbird family."

Brantley was now on a knee and peering over the crest of the hill. "Well," he said, "there's a Merriam's gobbler—part of the wild turkey family—that needs killing right down there."

I crawled up and peeked into the draw below where a longbeard was spinning in circles in the shade of a hackberry grove.

The two other toms were deflated and milling among the hens. Brantley and I both surveyed the lay of the land and pondered the situation for a while, but he beat me to the punch.

"What we need to do is crawl up that ditch with a fan."

"No, no," I said. "We need to circle out ahead of them."

"We can kill him from the ditch," he said.

"Brantley, we've been chasing these birds from behind for two hours, and every time we get close, they move on."

"Yeah, but they've got shade now, and we've got a ditch to crawl in."

I started to argue, but he raised a hand. "You know, Hurteau, what we really need to do is figure out which one of us is in charge here."

"I am, obviously," I said.

And he said, "Okay, ditch it is."

Brantley crawled out just ahead of me with the fan, and I followed with the shotgun. When we reached the end of the ditch, he lifted a rangefinder. Fifty-one yards. There was no getting closer, and the boss bird was starting to look nervous. I had a decision to make. I could take a long shot. Or I could pass—no one would blame me—and we could back out, circle ahead, and kill the bird my way. Then I could milk the remainder of that perfect spring day reminding Brantley that my plan was right and his was, well, close.

I would have been magnanimous about it, too. I would have said, "Don't worry about it, Brantley. It was *almost* a good idea." And "I'm sure the ditch will be a little longer next time."

Instead, I raised the gun, aimed, and dropped the tom where he stood, and Brantley wrote a feature story in *F&S* about how to crawl ditches with a fan for big spring gobblers.

We've been arguing about one thing or another ever since, and the question of who's in charge is still very much in play. Meanwhile,

Brantley's writing has gotten so good that about the only thing left for me to do now as an editor is delete the curse words.

It doesn't hurt that Brantley lives in a place where you can catch giant bass and slab crappies, noodle catfish, bowfish carp, and chase squirrels and ducks and spring gobblers and monster bucks all on half a tank of gas. It hurts even less that he does all these things with his wife, Michelle, and their boy, Anse, who are frequent and colorful characters in his stories. It especially helps that Michelle is smarter, tougher, and more country than him (don't mess with Michelle) and that Anse is more eaten up with the outdoors than either of them. But it's Brantley's talent as a writer that brings it all together.

Early on, we'd pegged Brantley as a how-to writer, an expert type. We weren't wrong, per se, as he can do that with the best of them. But with columns like "Beavercue" and "Bullfrogs in Aunt Tammy's Shit Pond" and with early features like "The Turkey Truants," "Lil's Last Hunt," "The Craig's List Camper," and "Baker's Thumb," we learned that Brantley's real gift is for a sort of diary-of-a-redneck storytelling that's unique in our space. Since we relaunched the print edition of *F&S* in 2024, this is what we've leaned on him for, and he's delivered with stories like "Trout Bums," "Old Trusty," "The Voodoo Box," and "Lockjaw"—his byline now regularly and rightly appearing alongside the David E. Petzals and Phil Bourjailys, the T. Edward Nickenses and Bill Heaveys. All of these stories (and many more) appear in this wonderful collection for you to take in and enjoy—and all of the curse words have been put back in.

As you read, maybe it will be helpful to know what I appreciate most about Brantley's writing, something quite rare and hard to pull off as a writer: it's that he never overdoes it. His writing is never tortured or flowery or overwrought. Many lesser writers try to elevate the outdoors with lofty prose. Not Brantley. He keeps it down in the mud and the blood and beer, to paraphrase Johnny

Cash (and in Brantley's case, that beer is definitely a Coor's Light). Some writers want to tell you what hunting and fishing is all about. Brantley just wants to tell you a story, maybe even a mildly crude one, and yet, somehow, what he has to say is no less poignant.

Okay, that's about enough of my singing Brantley's praises—except one last little story. Years ago, when Brantley was probably still in his twenties, I traveled to his home in Kentucky for our annual compound bow test. Brantley had just moved out of town to a new house on the hill, and his buddy Danny was busting his chops about it. "Damn, what are you paying this guy?" he asked me. "I know it isn't what the average outdoor writer makes."

"Well, I hate to say this with him sitting right there and all," I answered, "but Brantley is not your average outdoor writer. He's the best young writer there is." More than a decade later, I think I can say that on this point, at least, I was absolutely right. Even Brantley might not argue with it. But if he wants to, he knows where to find me.

—Dave Hurteau, executive editor, *Field & Stream*

Introduction

Mom and Dad had a small, built-in Formica table in their kitchen that they called "the bar." Even though there was a larger, nicer table not 6 feet away from it in the dining room, the bar was where we ate most of our meals, and it's also where my dad and his hunting buddies would sit after coming home from the woods. They'd sip whiskey, chew tobacco, smoke, and tell stories.

Some of my earliest memories of life are from there at that bar, when I was four or five years old. I believe it's where my education in storytelling began. Writing about hunting and fishing has been my primary job for my entire adult life, and it's taken me to 35 states, all over Canada, and to Mexico, Argentina, and New Zealand. When people hear that, they often ask, "How in the hell did you get a job like that?"

I could say that it all began at the bar. But more than that, it began with a compulsion to be outside. I grew up near Dawson Springs, Kentucky, and was one of a graduating class of 29 kids. I was a decent student, but not top of the class. I ran cross-country but wasn't a star and had no athletic skills otherwise. But I hunted for whatever was in season and fished for whatever would bite. Sometimes the fish wouldn't bite, and so I'd shoot them with a bow and arrow or spear them with a gig. In my early twenties, I learned to grab them by hand. Catfish noodling came naturally to me, and it suited me just fine.

Only at night, assuming I wasn't frog hunting, would I settle in and read. The late 1990s was the heyday of hunting and fishing magazines, and I collected them by the stack: *Game & Fish*, *Buckmasters*, *Outdoor Life*, *Field & Stream*, and *Guns & Ammo*. I remember noticing bylines above the stories and having some revelation that people actually got paid to write that stuff. I decided that's what I wanted to do myself.

Many of the magazines that inspired me as a kid were fizzling to an end just about the time I was getting into this profession. To make it as a hook-and-bullet writer required producing volumes of "how-to" stories for the internet, like "10 Ways to Shoot Bigger Bucks" and "The 5 Best Stinkbaits for Catfish." And it didn't hurt to supplement with other work on the side, from video editing to podcasting. I've done all of the above and worked as a hunting guide, too.

But there is still room for storytelling, and that's what this book is about, although I've sprinkled in some commentary as well because hunters and anglers all have opinions, and I like sharing mine as much as anyone. The stories I've included in this book are all true to the best of my memory, but I have changed the names of some of the people and places and have taken some liberties on dialogue since I can't always recall exactly what was said 20 or 30 years ago.

Most of these stories were originally published in *Field & Stream*, but others appeared in places such as Realtree.com, *Petersen's Hunting*, and *Game & Fish*. A few have long lived in my head but have never been written down until now. The book follows a loose timeline, beginning with childhood and ending in the present. The stories aren't perfectly organized chronologically, but they're close.

Any new hunting season begins with an opener. And so that's how we'll begin this story.

Chapter One
The Opener

Shagbarks

The old cabin had one room and a wood-burning stove, and getting to it used to require walking across an oak log that had fallen across Piney Creek. Erma-Granny—that was Dad's mom—slipped and fell off that log once, right into the creek, but it was warm, and she didn't panic. Erma-Granny was old and forgetful but tough, too, being one of 17 children who'd grown up during the Depression. She dog-paddled to the bank, where Dad helped her back onto the log. Then she crossed it, and we went on up the hill to the cabin, where she laughed about the fall and ate dinner and then crossed the log again in the dark.

We've long since cut roads into the place, but the old cabin itself hasn't changed much. It sits in a good spot, facing south with the creek bottom and softwoods to the west and hardwood ridges to the east. There's a grove of shagbark hickory trees on one of the ridges, and one August morning when I was seven years old, I followed Dad up to them toward a sound that was like rain, even though it was during the driest part of late summer, when the katydids sing at night.

Gray squirrels were making the racket as they chewed through the green husks of ripening hickory nuts, the "rain" being cuttings falling from the canopy. I was armed with a single-shot .22 rifle, a Remington Model 514 bolt-action. The bead was broken on the front sight, and the extractor on the bolt didn't work, either. After each shot, the spent rimfire case had to be manually pried out of the chamber, usually with the blade of a pocketknife. The rifle was a piece of junk to tell the truth of it, but it was a real gun, and being allowed to carry it at seven years old was something.

Not that I was much threat with it; I was only marginally better armed with the 514 than I would've been with a slingshot. Dad had encouraged me to squirrel hunt with a shotgun instead, insisting that killing squirrels with a load of No. 6 lead was much easier than trying to line up broken iron sights and connect with a single hollow-point bullet. But shotguns were big and loud, and the one time I'd fired one in the yard, it had kicked so hard that I lost my balance and skinned my thumb knuckle with the action release lever.

Dad didn't tell me to toughen up and use the shotgun anyway, but he did let the disparity between his scattergun and my rifle speak for itself. When we'd find a tree full of squirrels, he'd give me the first crack at them with the .22. But after I missed—which I always did—he'd shoulder his 16-gauge and go to work, tumbling the squirrels from the treetops. By the time I'd pried the spent .22 casing from the gun and reloaded, the action was usually over, with some squirrels dead on the ground and the escapees already out of range.

"Maybe I got one of them?" I'd ask, hopefully.

"Nope," he'd say. "I killed them all. There's not a .22 bullet hole through any of them."

But on that morning, before Dad started shooting, two young gray squirrels came spiraling out of the shagbark and down the trunk, engaged in some fierce dispute, their claws clicking and rattling against the loose bark. One of them stopped on a low limb, pulled itself into a neat little ball, and began chewing on a nut, its teeth scraping loud enough to be heard from 75 yards.

Dad didn't need to say much; I could see the squirrel less than 20 yards away, and it was the best shot opportunity I'd ever had. The Remington had a twist-type safety on the rear of the bolt, and I'd already turned it so that I could see the red portion, meaning the gun was ready to fire. I aimed and squeezed the trigger, and the bullet hit the squirrel with a *plop*. It fell instantly off the low limb.

Dad pulled his shotgun to his shoulder and began firing then, spitting out high-brass green hulls and replacing them with fresh shells in a practiced motion. The 16-gauge isn't popular these days, but he favored it back then for squirrels and quail especially. That gun, a single-barrel Model 37 Winchester that he called "Brother Win," threw a vicious pattern. Once we were within 20 yards of a tree's trunk, squirrels had to jump a lot of limbs before they were out of range.

We had a mess of squirrels (a "mess" is a loose unit of measure, probably best described as a few short of a legal limit). "That's enough to make a skillet stink," Dad said. "And you got that one." Sure enough, one of those squirrels was dead from a .22 bullet through the midsection. Dad wanted to put the squirrel in his game bag with the others, but I refused, instead carrying the critter by the tail with one hand and the Remington rifle with the other. We passed the old cabin on our hike down the ridge, and all the way back to the foot log, I rehearsed a hunting story in my head that I would go on to tell for years to anyone who would listen.

THE LESSON OF THE SHATTERED NIPPLE
The box under the Christmas tree was wrapped in colorful paper and shaped in such a long and slender way that inside there could've only been a boat paddle or a rifle. It was 1991. I was nine years old and hoping above all else to get my very first gun, one that I could 100 percent call my own, for Christmas. One heft of the box told me that whatever was inside was too heavy to be a paddle.

What I was expecting was a new .22 rifle. Dad had a cabinet full of guns, including .22s and 20-gauge shotguns, that he'd already been letting me carry when I was out squirrel hunting with him. But it had been made clear that all of those guns were his, and I technically couldn't claim that I owned a real gun of my own. On this Christmas morning, it seemed that was about to change.

But instead of a new .22, I unwrapped a sidelock .50-caliber muzzleloader. "I wanted to get you something you could deer hunt with," Dad said. "And I thought you might learn something with a gun like this, too."

I'd never been deer hunting and, moreover, had never so much as touched Dad's muzzleloader, a .50-caliber Thompson-Center Hawken replica. I remember when inline guns, sabots, and pelletized powder took over muzzleloader seasons, but this was before all of that. In those days, the late 1980s and early 1990s, black-powder hunters used percussion guns with open sights, loose black powder, and patched round balls. It was a specialized, 50-yard sport, and Dad particularly enjoyed the process of it all.

"Every deer I've ever hit with a black powder fell dead on the spot," he'd tell me. "A .50-caliber rifle is a lot of gun, but we'll start with light charges so it won't kick the shit out of you."

The gun broke on the very first shot. We'd measured out a 60-grain charge of FFG black powder and loaded a round ball, and I fired it at a board that we'd leaned against a tree maybe 15 yards away. I missed the board clean, shaking like I was. Dad pulled the gun's hammer back to half-cock to flick away the spent cap, and that's when we noticed the problem. In all the black-powder shooting Dad had done previously and in the thousands of rounds of it that I've done since, I've never seen anything like it. The nipple, on which the percussion cap is placed to ignite the powder charge in the breech below, broke as if it were a shattered piece of glass. It was maybe a $3 part that could be replaced in 20 seconds, but it was absolutely required for the gun to work. And on Christmas morning, we had no replacement.

Despite the man-size gift, I was crying a child's tears. Dad hustled inside, grabbed his "possibles" bag from the hunting closet, and removed the nipple from his own Hawken with a special wrench. "See, it's an easy thing to fix," he said, confident he'd found the solution to save his boy's Christmas. But the threads on the two guns were different. We had to clean my new muzzleloader, rendered to the usefulness of a heavy, sinking boat paddle, and put it in the cabinet on Christmas morning after just one shot.

A small box with a dozen replacement nipples—some for my gun, some for Dad's Hawken—soon arrived in the mail. I killed my first deer with that muzzleloader the next fall, and I hunted with it for the next decade before finally retiring it in favor of a scoped inline. It's always been kept clean, and it still shoots straight.

Dad hoped I'd learn from that muzzleloader, and I guess I have. These days, I'm not a guy who overpacks ahead of a hunt. But I do keep an extra rifle and ammo in the truck. Another duck call in my blind bag. An extra release aid in my bowhunting pack. Two knives. Two flashlights. A copy of my license. I back up the stuff I must have to finish a hunt. Sometimes, on Christmas morning, your nipple will shatter, and without a replacement handy, you're up a creek. But at least you'll have a paddle.

Bullfrogs in Aunt Tammy's Sh*t Pond

A good hunter can identify a trophy bullfrog from across a 2-acre pond just by looking at the size of its eyes and the spacing between them in the beam of a flashlight. It's a skill learned from experience. That experience will further teach you that once you've gotten close enough to really see a mature frog, you realize it's something of a disturbing creature: big enough to eat a half-grown hamster, bound in muscle, and green skin and black eyes. Were your buddy to say, *Grab him!*, you might hesitate.

Bullfrogs start calling in the late spring once the poison ivy is about 4 inches tall and the carpenter bees are buzzing around the rafters of the barn. All of that signals the start to summer, and it happens in early May in my part of the world. The best bullfrog hunt I've ever had occurred on a humid night at about that time of year, 30 years ago, with Dan, my best buddy at the time.

He and I didn't attend the same school, and there was no texting or social media then, so our weekend plans were always made carefully over the phone during the week prior. For that frogging mission, we'd stay at his grandmother's house, a mile down a gravel road from a pond that Dan had been scouting. We'd leave out just after nightfall. We carried nothing electronic except for Dan's D-cell Maglite. We were two boys entrusted to walk into the woods after dark, with spears, and then simply come home when we were finished killing frogs.

I carried an old gig fastened on the end of a broom handle. It was missing two tines, but the three it had left had been filed and honed to a fine point. Dan was packing the artillery: a spring-loaded contraption on the end of a collapsible aluminum pole that he called a *snap gig*. Had you been able to anchor those jaws to the ground, they might've sufficed for a foot-hold bear trap. Dan had to stand on one jaw to cock the snap gig, and then just to prove it'd work as designed, he jabbed it against an oak sapling. It snapped shut violently, and it required the both of us to pry the thing loose. Dan seemed pleased. *"Put that against a frog, and you've got him,"* he said. *"My pawpaw said so."*

After a long, mostly silent march through the dark, we stepped off the gravel road and into the trees. Even without lights, the deep *barrummphs* of amorous male frogs would've led us right to the pond.

"What is this place?" I whispered.

"It's my Aunt Tammy's shit pond," Dan said. "You wait till you see the frogs in here."

Indeed, Dan's Aunt Tammy bred rottweilers for a living; during the day, a low-flying plane would set the yard full of dogs to howling. And rottweilers are big animals; even an individual one produces enough large piles of waste in a year's time that its disposal has to be considered, just in the general day-to-day ownership of the animal. But a rottweiler *dealership*, so to speak, needs a place all its own, purely to get rid of poop. For Aunt Tammy, that place was in a little pond out in the woods.

Dan had gotten word that there were frogs in that pond, and he'd scouted it one night just before the season opened. When you go frog listening, a good rule of thumb is to assume that for every frog you can hear calling in a pond, there's at least another gigging-sized one sitting nearby but keeping quiet. In this pond, Dan said he heard a dozen frogs. Maybe more.

He wasn't lying. He turned on the light and shined it across the pond. It betrayed the glowing eyes of bullfrogs surrounding the shoreline. They'd grown large in the pond, which seemed void of tadpole-eating fish. We started out walking the bank, holding the Maglite on a frog and trying to spear it from behind, but for every frog we killed, we'd jump several others. It was frustrating, like chasing a dangled carrot that's never quite within reach.

After a while, we turned off the light, sat in the dark for a bit, and waited for the frogs to climb back onto shore. Then we dared one another to step off the bank and wade into the pond. Soon, we were both easing through water and muck up to our armpits—but the strategy worked; we were able to shine Dan's light right at the frogs and attack them from the water, like lurking gators. Dan carried a Ka-Bar survival knife, and we took turns with the gigs. One of us would jab at a frog, dig into the mud with bare hands to grasp it about the waist, and then present it to the other. That person would use the big knife to sever the frog's legs at the pelvis with a crunch and a squish, drop them into a grocery sack, and then shuck the front half of the frog off the gig and into the shit pond. It was brutal work, but we seemed made for it.

It took two sacks to carry all the frog legs home, but we hauled them in the dark, tennis shoes sloshing and us both soaked from the armpits down in the shit pond. I don't know who killed the biggest frog or the most of them. I do know that when we added our piles of legs together and Dan's grandmother fried them up for breakfast, it seemed like we couldn't eat enough of them to find the plate underneath.

Lockjaw
One day this monster bass swam by me. I was bluegill fishing at the time. I cut off my bluegill rig and tied on an Original Rapala Minnow. It didn't take but 1 cast and 30 seconds to lose the Rapala & fish.
—Handwritten by a 13-year-old, April 1996

I had been waiting for a bluegill to sink my red-and-white bobber when the bass, nearly 2 feet long, swam down the shoreline at my feet. Just about all strip-mine lakes are clear, and the Bass Hole—that was the name of this pit—was so clear that I could see the half-inch piece of nightcrawler hanging on the hook beneath my bobber, cast 20 feet out from the shoreline.

The bass was much closer, gliding through the water but somehow also seeming motionless, an ambush predator that had perfected its art. I'd never seen such a fish. In fact, it was only the spring prior when I'd fished the Bass Hole for the first time and caught my first real bass. I'd hooked some little largemouths on worms while bluegill fishing before, but that had been kid stuff. That first day at the Bass Hole, Dad had handed me a Rebel Crawdad crankbait and told me to tie it on, cast it out, and reel it in pretty fast, with a twitch every now and then. I threw it near a log, and as soon as the lure touched down, a 15-inch largemouth clobbered it. I begged Dad to get that fish mounted, but he said it wasn't big enough. We fried it instead.

But the fish at my feet, I knew, was something for a taxidermist. I cranked in my bluegill rig about fast enough to start a friction fire and cut it off with a pocketknife, just above the bobber. I dropped the whole thing—bobber, sinker, hook, flaccid piece of crawler, and 3-foot length of 8-pound Stren—onto the ground. I was standing on a point that was maybe 10 feet wide and one of only two good casting spots on the banks of the Bass Hole, the rest of the pit's shoreline being nearly vertical and lined with trees. To my left, where the bank got steep again, was an old beaver hut, and I watched the bass turn and settle itself in front of that.

I had a few good bass plugs in my tackle box—a Rebel Crawdad, of course; a Hula Popper; and a 2-inch Rapala Minnow among them. I chose the Minnow and fired a cast toward the beaver hut. I twitched the lure maybe twice before the bass grabbed it, evidenced by the white flash of a giant bucket mouth.

The Opener

It then swam nearly the same course along the shoreline where I'd spotted it earlier, just a bit farther out from the bank and with my lure stuck to its face.

But the fish didn't seem to be especially panicked; more annoyed. The bass simply eased toward deeper water, loading the rod as it went. Me, I *was* panicked, and I ruined the opportunity almost immediately. I clawed for the reel handle and tried to turn it, but there was a crack, not unlike the sound of a .22 rifle, loaded with Shorts. The end of the rod quivered for a second or two before settling, and loose monofilament flapped on the surface of the water, like a bit of ash swirling after a hot fire. The bass and my Rapala Minnow plug both were gone.

One day, I had Matt Seymore over and Lockjaw was sighted. Along with her smaller sister. After multiple lures were thrown, the fish earned the name "Lockjaw." So, I went back to bluegill fishing. Who should take my worm under but Lockjaw? Once again she was saved by light line.
—June 1996

The details of a fishing story usually get fuzzier with age—but not with this story, even 30 years later. There's no doubt that the exact lure the fish stole was a Rapala Minnow, for example, just as there's no doubt it broke off my Rebel Crawdad a few days later, when I was standing on the same little 10-foot flat and casting toward the beaver hut. And there's no doubt still that I was "outfitted with a Quantum QL3 light spinning rod and reel combo" and that I knew, even at age 13, that I was underequipped to land a fish like that.

All of it is recorded in the journal that I used to keep, under a special entry that I penned in early June 1997 called "The Tale of Lockjaw." That fish story recapped a series of events that began in the spring of 1996—when I lost the bass for the first time on the minnow plug. I even drew a picture of the lost plug, and the crawdad plug that I lost after it, in the notebook's margin.

Back then, I didn't get paid by the word, so I kept the details succinct. The journal was a spiral notebook that had entries on my first turkey and my first quail and a lot about the bird dogs I used to hunt with almost every day. I even had hand-drawn maps marking where I'd found coveys of quail within walking distance of the house, and looking at them now reminds me of just how long ago it's all been. All of those birds have been gone for decades, and all of that land is long since leased up and posted.

An entry from January 31, 1999, reads, *"Today was the last day of quail and rabbit season. This year sucked terribly. I may take up duck hunting next year."*

I had also drawn a map of the best strip-mine lakes in the area. There was the Bass Hole and the Swimming Hole, the Trash Pit, Bud's Pit, Bobby's Pit, Pecker Bass Lake, and plenty of others. This was in the reclaimed strip mines of western Kentucky, one of the top coal-producing areas in the state. Much of the land was owned or leased by mining companies in those days, and the rest of it was owned by neighbors who, if I didn't know, I knew of.

I roamed the place on foot, fishing tackle in hand. I had no concept of property lines out there, and neither did any of the other country kids whom I'd run into on occasion, sometimes out fishing themselves but usually smoking pot and jumping off the cliff into the deep waters of the Swimming Hole. The cliff was actually a high wall, left over from the mining operation, and some of the kids had spray-painted the words "Mount Bitch" onto the face.

I caught some nice fish at the Swimming Hole, too, but usually I hiked on farther to the Bass Hole, where I almost never saw anyone else. And after I'd broken off the enormous fish, not once but twice, the decision on where to go fishing on any given day was easy. I had buddies who would sometimes walk to the pit with me, where we'd then argue over who would stand in which spot. My buddy Matt Seymore was with me the day we gave the legendary bass its name.

It never occurred to us at the time that the fish's "smaller sister" was probably a male bass and that the two were likely spawning and therefore not interested in the crankbaits and spinnerbaits and plastic worms that Seymore and I pounded them with for 100 casts straight. We settled on "Lockjaw" before the fish finally pulled my bluegill rig under and snapped me off again.

After that, I'd sit awake at night, thinking of that particular bass and how I might catch it. I'd have no more entertained the idea of there being more than one lunker bass in that pit worthy of a name than Captain Ahab would've entertained the idea of several white whales swimming about. The dog-day heat of late summer baked in, and the fishing got slow, and soon enough, it was hunting season again. But still, over the long winter, I wondered, *Why had that bass hit the bluegill rig after ignoring everything else?*

And then it hit me. It didn't bite the bluegill rig. It bit at a little bluegill that was messing with the worm.

Turkey season has definitely been a great one. We have called in 18 birds over the course of the season. This morning, I dropped my second turkey. He came off the roost like he was on a string. I busted him at 30 yards.
—April 1997

It was early May of the following summer when I started thinking about fishing again. Turkey season had just ended, and I'd filled my tag on the last day of April. I hiked to the Bass Hole one afternoon, carrying my usual backpack with tackle, along with a Walmart sack in case I found morel mushrooms. I also had two spinning rods and a metal coffee can. I had a bluegill rig tied to one of the rods and a 1/0 worm hook on the Quantum. I began filling a stringer with big, hump-headed bream, and I sloughed a few little sunnies into the coffee can, which I'd filled with pit water.

As I watched my bobber, I stood on the flat and also scanned the shallows, especially over toward the beaver dam. Soon enough,

Lockjaw emerged from under the dam, and by the time I'd grabbed one of the bluegills out of the coffee can and threaded it onto the worm hook, just under the dorsal fin, the bass was again at my feet.

I wasn't prepared for just how far a live bluegill could be cast on a long and limber spinning rod, and so I overshot the bass by a good 20 feet. The bluegill hit the surface with a slap, and I pulled it toward the bass, which, instead of spooking, had spun toward the hooked baitfish and was writhing its fins, like a goldfish awaiting a pinch of food.

The bluegill scarcely settled before that great white mouth flashed again. This time, I felt ready, having adjusted my drag to slip. But when the fish made its run, the amount of line peeling off my reel startled me—and I tightened the drag back up. There was that familiar .22-esque crack again. Fourteen-year-old me would've never admitted to crying over a fish, not even to Matt Seymore, but that's exactly what I did. I sat on that flat and cried for a good while.

I am now convinced that spinning reels are evil. —May 1997

Our neighbor Ronnie was a close friend who'd grown up fishing many of the same pits himself. He also had a wall full of mounted trophy bass and would sometimes counsel me on the best approaches for any given day. Wintertime, you didn't expect much, but you fished a hair jig with a piece of pig on the back. A Mann's Augertail worm was always a good choice, especially when smeared with a gob of Smelly Jelly. And *Son, in a pit like that, he's got to eat every day. You want to catch him, you've got to go fishing.*

After losing the bass again, Ronnie asked what kind of rod and reel I was using. When I told him, he did not seem at all sympathetic, like I'd also told him that I still believed in the Easter Bunny. "Got-damn, son, it's time to grow up. You need to go look through your daddy's tackle and learn to use one of his baitcasters," he said.

The Opener

Dad indeed had some baitcasters that he never used because he always believed that you'd catch more fish with lighter gear, and he was probably right. But he also had the grown man's presence of mind and patience to slowly fight a big bass on spinning gear, letting the drag do the work.

Lockjaw had proven that I had no such patience. I didn't ask Dad but instead just went to looking, and I found a pair of Ambassadeur 5000s on wooden, pistol-grip rods that were dusty and spooled with brittle old line. But Dad also had a fresh spool of 17-pound-test, and so I took one of the casting reels, wound on fresh line, and tied on a weight that I'd cut off a duck decoy, which I figured was more or less as heavy as a small live bluegill. Rigged as such, I stepped into the backyard and practiced pitching it. Within a few tries, I learned to prevent overruns by thumbing the spool, and within 20 minutes, I figured I could manage a 20-foot cast.

I tied a bluegill rig onto my spinning rod and another big worm hook onto the baitcaster. And on May 18, 1997, I went fishing again at the Bass Hole, with my backpack as always and the coffee can. I didn't fish for long. I'd put two sunnies into the can when I saw Lockjaw lumber into the shadows under the dam. I took the baitcaster, put one of the small bream on the hook, and scooted along the steep bank above the dam. I couldn't see the bass at first, but as the ripples settled after tossing the bluegill, I saw it approaching like a black missile and then the familiar white flash of its giant mouth.

This time, when the bass ran and the rod loaded, I pulled back hard—and immediately spun the fish's head toward me.

I took one of my dad's baitcasters with 17-pound line. I used bluegill, and this time, I horsed Lockjaw from a beaver dam. I took her a good 50 yards up the bank. Then I unhooked her. —May 1997

The banks of the pit being so steep, I was afraid to set the fish down for fear it would flop all the way back to the water. So, I ran around and carried it, tightly held with both hands on the lower jaw and whooping the whole way, like the other kids bailing off Mount Bitch. I pulled the morel sack from my backpack and stashed the bass inside, and that's how I got it home, flopping in a grocery sack with my having to switch arms every so often because it was so heavy. Mom later drove me down the road so I could show the bass to Ronnie.

"That one's 6 or 7 pounds all day," he said. Although I never actually weighed Lockjaw with a scale or anything, I took his lead—and a few liberties in the journal.

She weighed in at 7 pounds, 3 ounces. She is waiting for the taxidermist in my freezer. —June 1997

I still have the skin mount of that fish, which I carried with me to college and hung in my first apartment and in several subsequent offices in the years since. Sometimes my son, now just a little younger than I was when I caught Lockjaw, asks me about it. I can't say that I've caught a bigger bass anywhere since. I'm not sure that I ever want to.

Trout Fishing with Kenny Dean

On my first morning in Calico Rock, Arkansas, I awoke to the sight and sound of Kenny Dean sitting on the toilet. The door to the motel room bathroom worked just fine, but it was as if the thought of taking his morning dump without an audience never crossed Kenny's mind. He was beaming from ear to ear and yelling at my dad, who was still asleep. "Jimmy! Jimmy, get up! We have to get this boy out there to go fishing," he said. "He's going to catch a big brown today, I just know it."

The Opener

At 14 years old, I didn't need any extra coaxing to get up and get dressed. Aside from Kenny's bowels, the room smelled like wet waders, 2-stroke outboard gas, whiskey, and whole kernel corn from where we'd fished the evening before. Calico Rock is a trout town, and the White River is home not only to an endless population of stocker rainbows but to some big brown trout as well. I'd caught my fill of the rainbows by then; what I wanted was a 5-pound brown trout to put on the wall. I retied the crankbait—a trout-colored Rapala Countdown Minnow—that I'd been casting the evening before. Kenny said that bait would work almost as well as anything to catch a big trout, and when it came to fishing, especially fishing in Arkansas, I trusted him over about everyone else.

Kenny was a lawyer—a good one, Dad said—but he usually had a johnboat hitched up to his old Chrysler, even when it was parked at the courthouse. When I was a kid, I thought of him mainly as a professional fisherman of sorts because I hadn't had many interactions with him that didn't somehow involve fishing. And fishing with Kenny Dean always came with an educational bonus. One time, while out on an overnight bluegill fishing and camping trip, he'd taught my little brother, Matt, six years old at the time, the seven different kinds of farts. Matt came home the next morning and recited them all—fizz, fuzz, fuzzy-wuzz, poot, tally-poot, tear-ass, and rattler—to my mom.

An overnight bream trip near the house was one thing. But a multiday adventure to the White River, clear in another state, was another. Kenny was the perfect guide since he'd grown up in Arkansas and he and Dad had taken the same trip several times before and had always come home with a cooler full of trout. But I didn't get to go because Mom said I was too young to be road-tripping with Kenny.

But that changed once I was 14, having proven that I was old enough to roam the strip-mine lakes alone and to fish with a baitcaster. Kenny told Dad that my "nuts were probably dropping," and I didn't know what that meant, but it seemed to be proof that I was old enough to go on a fishing trip with the men. Once on the road, Kenny never let up with the stories. At one point, he'd nearly convinced me that he was my real father.

"Jesus, Kenny, can you just take a breath?" Dad finally said to him. He was driving and seemed to be craving a moment's silence.

Kenny laughed. "I'm just teasing about that, son, I could never be your real dad because your mother couldn't stand me," he said. Then he looked at Dad. "Jimmy, are we going to eat dinner at that restaurant with the pool tables again this year?"

Dad shook his head, and Kenny turned back to me.

"It's a great place, Will, we'll take you there," he said. "We had a big time last year. You see, your daddy, your real daddy, is a good pool player. After we got done fishing last summer, we stopped at the restaurant to eat, and they had a table. I racked 'em up to play a game of 8-ball, and this big fat woman came up, slapped her hand by the corner pocket, and said, 'That's *my* table.' Course, I didn't see her damn name on it."

Dad spoke up, never taking his eyes off the road. "And that's exactly what Kenny said to her. *I don't see your damn name on it.* Everything got worse."

"What happened?" I asked.

"Kenny told her we'd been fishing down at the river," Dad said, "then he looked her square in the eyes and asked if she'd been fishing down there, too, or if she just smelled that way all the time."

Kenny howled in hysterics over his own antics. "I'll tell you what, son, she had a good sense of humor. She played your daddy in a game of 8-ball, and he beat her big ass fair and square."

We hit the river that day with half a dozen spinning rods—rigged with either crankbaits or corn spinners—along with Dad's fly rod, which mostly lay unused on the floor of the boat. Kenny brought along several cans of Beenie Weenie, too, because he was prone to getting low blood sugar, and he said that Beenie Weenie was the surest of all cures for that.

It was 90 degrees by noon, and we had close to a limit of trout. Dad tied the boat up in the shade of a river bend to eat lunch. The White's modest current kept the boat swaying gently against the rope. Kenny leaned back in his seat and sang, "Under the shade of the beech nut tree, little Will Brantley there sat. He was amusing himself by . . ."

"Kenny!" Dad interrupted. "You don't have to teach him that song."

Kenny just smiled. Not five minutes later, he whispered the remainder of the tune into my ear and made me commit it to memory. I'd never heard anything so crude. "You take that back and teach it to all the other boys in your class, just like you did with the seven kinds of farts," he said.

Later that night, the room again smelled like wet waders and farts and trout slime. Dad and Kenny were kicked back on the motel beds, sipping whiskey from the same stainless Thermos lids that they'd used for coffee cups that morning and tobacco spitters at midday. Exhausted from the casting and the sun, I turned on the sink to brush my teeth, took in a mouth full of water, and immediately spit it out.

"Sweet Jesus," I said. "That water tastes terrible! Dad, I'm going have to wash my mouth out with some of that whiskey."

Kenny belted out his signature laugh. "Whew, boy, I'm glad it's not my son talking like that!"

Dad smiled, but cautiously. "No, he's mine. And he's not getting any whiskey or going down to the pool hall."

Those things would have to come later. But at 14, what I did get was to go trout fishing for the first time, learn a little extra from Kenny Dean, and be allowed to sit and talk and laugh among the men.

Joe's Pheasant

Joe and his brother Dub ran a farm and a sawmill at the dead end of a gravel road a couple miles from where I grew up. Dad knew the brothers well and had hunted their place for years, mostly for quail. Joe and Dub would let about anyone hunt as long as they stopped and asked, but their place wasn't easy to find, and so not many people stopped and asked. When you did catch them outside, Dub would stand and talk, but Joe never had much to say, even when the sawmill wasn't running. He was an army veteran who had worked on oil rigs and in the coal mines in his younger years.

Joe's house was right next to the main gate into the farm, and if he happened to be outside when I came through to hunt, I'd sheepishly remind him that I was Jim Brantley's son and was hoping to go hunting. He'd say, "Go ahead," if he spoke at all. As often as not, he'd just grunt and nod at the gate and then redirect his attention toward whatever lumber needed sawing at the moment. Joe or Dub—I can't remember which one—was missing a finger or two. Maybe it was from a sawmill, but there are lots of other things on the farm, and in the army and the coal mines and oil rigs, that can claim fingers.

But that permission to hunt was a golden ticket because paradise awaited beyond the gate. The property was just the type of small patchwork farm that you'd expect of the day, a couple hundred acres of fencerows grown thick with blackberry briars and little cornfields that were worked with a tractor and old-fashioned disk weighed down with logs. The hillsides were full of white oaks and hickories, and a few cattle milled about, though you might hunt a half day without seeing any of them.

I shot my first quail there, hunting with Dad and his dogs, and a few turkeys over the years, too. But the bottomland cornfields next to Bull Creek really captivated me. They'd flood reliably after a big rain, and then ducks would hit them. Dad wasn't much of a duck hunter, and we weren't in much of a duck spot, and so the chance to hunt those birds was a real treat to me, something I'd mostly only read about in hunting magazines. Dad had half a dozen plastic mallard decoys that were rigged with lag bolts, fishing sinkers, and assorted scrap metal for weights and stored in a horse feed sack.

One winter when I was 16, we got a rain heavy enough for Bull Creek to flood. Once the storm passed and the sky broke clear and cold, I made plans to go duck hunting. I loaded my gear—the feed sack of decoys and Dad's Browning B-80—onto a four-wheeler and rode through Joe's gate in the predawn, switching off the headlight as I approached his house, just to be sure I didn't wake anyone up. The sawmill was silent there in the dark, and a sprinkling of frost had gathered on the gate. I closed it behind me and rode on down the dirt road along a ridge spine that followed a pasture that was just below Joe's house. I don't know if Joe was a coffee drinker, but assuming he was, I expect he often stood at the window of his house and looked out over the pasture below with a cup in hand. It was a nice view.

I rode the path until it dropped off into the bottoms, into acres of cornstalks that were flooded just deep enough to make the place look ducky. I parked the four-wheeler under a dry tree, filled my pockets with Double-X magnum steel shotgun shells, and waded into the water, wearing a leaky pair of neoprene waders and carrying the feed sack of decoys in one hand and the shotgun in the other.

One of the fencerows, flooded, made for a good place to squat and hide. I tossed the decoys out maybe 20 yards away, kneeled, and waited for daylight. The sky softened, and ducks swarmed overhead like mosquitoes. I shot and missed and reloaded and shot and cussed and finally knocked down a black duck and two wood ducks. The melee may have lasted 20 minutes, and I probably could've killed more ducks had I waited—but I had half a limit and really couldn't wait to tell somebody about it.

It was early, probably still coffee-drinking time, when I was back on the four-wheeler and driving back up the dirt path, through the pasture and on my way home. I saw the pheasant as I topped the ridge spine, within view of the gate and Joe's house. That a gaudy rooster was standing there was unusual for a few reasons. Pheasants don't live in Kentucky, for one. And most critters that do live in Kentucky know to haul ass when they see a 16-year-old boy riding a four-wheeler with a shotgun.

But this pheasant was standing stock still on the highest point of the ridge, orange and green and splendid, like a painting. I figured he was an escapee from a game farm, and I knew it was legal to shoot him—plus, he'd be a delicious complement to my ducks. I stopped the four-wheeler and sat idling to formulate a plan to get within range, and that's when the pheasant lowered its head and began toward me at a trot, not breaking stride once until it was only 50 yards away. Then it stretched and crowed—*cawww-caw*—flitting its wings rapidly in a display that startled me because I'd never seen it but also tripped something predatory because it reminded me a good bit of a gobbling turkey.

I slid the B-80 out of the gun case and thumbed one of the few shotgun shells I had left into the magazine. The pheasant eyed me, suspicious, but since it didn't seem afraid of the four-wheeler, I decided to give it a little gas and ease closer. Fifty yards with a shotgun is a long way.

The bird then lowered its head and charged, covering green pasture ground as only a determined gallinaceous bird can. I've seen spooked turkeys run that fast and sometimes bobwhite quail when crossing the road in the spring. But those birds had always been going the other way. Before I could rack the shell into the chamber of the B-80, the pheasant was standing alongside the four-wheeler, crowing up at me.

I should've known that wasn't normal behavior for a pheasant, even a game farm escapee, but by then, I was intent on frying the bird and having it with some gravy, and maybe Mom would make some good canned biscuits. But if 50 yards had been too far for a Double-X magnum duck load, 3 yards was too close. It occurred to me that if I got off the four-wheeler slowly, maybe I could catch the bird.

I dismounted, and the pheasant cocked its eye up and sideways to study me. When I lunged, the bird sidestepped my attempt as deftly as a prize fighter, running just a few feet ahead toward Joe's house before stopping again.

And I followed it, but I wasn't that agile, seeing as how I was still wearing soggy chest waders and clutching Dad's prized Browning, which I'd yet to fully load. The pheasant would allow me to walk almost to within grabbing distance before sprinting ahead and stopping again, never more than 10 yards away, crowing for every two or three attempts I made. I chased the bird for a while until both of us were virtually in the shadow of Joe's house, just beyond the gate, with the four-wheeler now more than 100 yards away.

I decided to trick the bird and win this chase. I turned my back and walked toward the four-wheeler, as if I was no longer at all interested. But as I stepped off 25 paces, I hit the magazine release on the B-80 and racked the duck load into the tube. I spun around, shouldered the shotgun as if firing a salute, and shot that pheasant dead. I stashed him in the feed sack, along with the decoys and my ducks, and rode through the gate and past Joe's house and the sawmill. I didn't see him or Dub, but it was cold, and I didn't figure they'd have the time to stand around and listen to a kid's hunting story anyway.

But I wasn't about to let Dad finish a full workday without telling him. I called his office and told him all about my ducks that morning in the flooded corn. "And then best of all, I got a big old rooster pheasant on my way home," I said. "He was standing in the pasture below Joe's house!"

Dad got quiet on the phone. "Shit," he finally said. "I went bird hunting there the other day, and Joe specifically said to not let my dogs get after his pet pheasant." My heart sank.

"Well, maybe this one was a different pheasant," I suggested. Dad didn't say anything. "I think I'm going to go back hunting in the bottoms this afternoon and see if I can get my other three ducks."

"If Joe asks about that pheasant, you better tell him," Dad said.

I left in plenty of time for an afternoon hunt, with pockets full of more duck loads. As I rode the four-wheeler down the gravel road and toward the gate, I could hear the buzz of the sawmill. Joe looked up as I neared him, slowed the four-wheeler to a stop, and shut off the key.

"Hey, Joe, I was going to go duck hunting in your bottoms down there this evening if that's okay."

"It's okay. Did you shoot my pheasant?"

There I sat on the four-wheeler, a scrawny 16-year-old kid, looking up at Joe, knowing that he could smash me with one hand even if it was missing some fingers and also knowing that I had to explain how I'd chased his pet pheasant down and then killed it with a shotgun when I couldn't catch it.

"Yes, sir, I did. And I'm sorry. I didn't know it was your pet until my dad told me. I just saw it in the pasture this morning when I was coming out and thought it must've been from a game farm. It came out . . ."

"I saw you down there chasing it," Joe said. "It came to your four-wheeler. We'd feed it off our four-wheeler, and it got used to the sound."

I was fresh out of useful things to say. "Well, I've got it soaking in salt water at home. Not a pellet mark on the meat if you want me to bring it back to you to eat."

"No. I don't want to eat it. We were just trying to get a few of them to raise down there. I liked looking at him. Go ahead and go duck hunting, be careful in that water," he said.

And then he turned and went back to his sawmill.

I found a game farm nearby with pheasants for sale. Maybe it's where the bird in question had been raised, I'm not sure. But I probably shouldn't have told the owner about my predicament because he laughed and also charged me a fortune for two roosters and two hens plus a wire cage to put them in. At 16, I didn't have a fortune to spend, but I did have a debt to pay.

It was midwinter, after duck season had ended but well before turkey season began, when I drove back down the dead-end road toward the sawmill. Dub was outside. "I brought you guys these pheasants," I said right away. The roosters and hens were in the cage with their heads tucked, their eyes covered by flight hoods. "It's two hens and two roosters. I killed the one, you know, and felt bad about it. So, I got you and Joe these."

Dub smiled and walked closer. "Boy, they pretty," he said. "We can put them over there in the chicken coop until they settle down."

I carried the cage toward the coop and then reached inside to get the nearest bird, a rooster. It flogged, spurring me across the palm of the hand, but I held on and stuffed it and the three others into the chicken coop. I would've liked it had Joe been there to see it all and maybe noticing the spur wound dripping blood on my palm, but Dub seemed pleased, and that had to be good enough. I left fast as I could.

Ringneck pheasants are a popular game bird but technically an invasive species to the United States, having been imported from China in the 1880s and released in the West. The birds thrive in open grasslands and have done particularly well in states like the Dakotas, Iowa, Nebraska, and Kansas. Although released pheasants can be found on some game farms in the South, self-sustaining populations have never been established successfully in places like Kentucky.

Nonetheless, Joe and Dub dutifully cared for the four pheasants that I'd bought for them with plans to release them. And in the early spring, they herded them into the wire cage I'd left, carried the cage out toward the pasture just below Joe's house, and opened the door.

I asked Joe that spring, when I rode up to go turkey hunting, how the pheasants were doing and if he ever heard them crowing and would they come to the four-wheeler like that first one.

"They flew off, and we never saw them again," he said. "You can turkey hunt if you want to."

And then he turned back to the lumber that needed sawing in his mill.

On BB Gun Safaris

We used to leave before daybreak on Saturday morning, groups of two or three boys, none of us old enough to drive. We walked into the woods, with no adult supervision to be found, during a time when cell phones didn't exist and ended up miles from home, crossing hayfields of farmers we didn't know or sitting on the banks of creeks we couldn't name. We rarely carried water, but we'd sometimes stash a lukewarm Sam's Choice cola in a backpack.

The expeditions were planned around our supplies of ammunition. We had cartons of Copperhead BBs and plastic boxes of .177 pellets, the pointed kind, if we were lucky enough to find them. We were armed with pump-up pellet rifles and CO_2 pistols. A package of five CO_2 cartridges could get you through a full weekend of hunting if you conserved your shots, but no kid who ever saved for a semiautomatic pellet pistol did so with the intent of conserving ammo. The gas went quickly, and so sometimes we'd pool money for a full case of 25 gas cartridges. The CO_2 had a smell, and the first few shots from a cartridge were always louder, more pungent, and more satisfying than the latter shots, and they hit harder, too. If you came across a squirrel, a rabbit, or a dove, you wanted to be loaded with a fresh cartridge and good, pointed pellets.

We shot at squirrels, rabbits, and doves but also at frogs, snakes, and a few things we weren't supposed to be shooting at. Dads and mothers were told that we shot blackbirds and nothing else. I can't condone everything those boys did—but I also know that we matured quickly and naturally adopted a fundamental code of right and wrong.

With a pellet gun in hand and a world to explore, I learned hunting skills that have served me to this day. I also created some of my best memories of childhood. I've shared camps with hundreds of other hunters in my lifetime, in this country and in others, and almost all of the most skillful ones spent their formative years exactly the same way: hunting on foot for birds and whatever else with a pellet gun.

Such a BB gun safari is more difficult for kids of today, of course. That's a shame when we consider all of the other things that seem to be conspiring to keep kids indoors: the screens, the schedules, and the helicopter parenting culture that seems averse to any risk, any failure, and anything uncomfortable.

Yet, as the father of a 10-year-old boy—one who loves to hunt and has a pellet gun of his own—it does seem like some of that parenting culture has been born of necessity. I'm not at all afraid of my son shooting his eye out with a BB; he's safer with a gun than many adults are. Nor am I afraid of him being bitten by a snake or eaten by a bear. But I am suspicious of other people. Out in the woods myself, I've run into characters I wouldn't want alone around my kid. My instincts tell me to be careful and protective.

And even in the safest of areas, attitudes about property lines have changed. I remember getting "caught" by farmers when I was a kid out kicking fencerows for rabbits or looking for pigeons around the barn. I once killed a farmer's pet pheasant—not realizing it was a pet because pheasants usually aren't—and fried it and ate it. While the farmer wasn't happy, he didn't scold me or send me home. He told me to go hunting and be careful.

But today, there are food plots and big buck core areas we don't want disturbed, and the farmer is afraid that Little Billy's helicopter mom will sue him if Billy breaks his ankle down at the creek. And of course there are the simple optics of it. A passerby seeing a group of kids carrying guns is likelier to call the law in 2024 than in 1994. And perhaps, given all that's happened since 1994, that's the best thing to do.

I understand all of these things, and I suppose I sound like an old man remembering his glory days. But none of that changes my opinion: the BB gun safaris of my childhood were a fine time. Kids of today would be better off if they got to enjoy them on occasion, too.

Chapter Two
Young Bucks

A Date with Some Deer Piss

Halloween is my favorite holiday. The October hardwoods are splendid, and the whitetail bucks are only days away from a full month of breeding hysterics. I enjoy the scary movies and venison chili that come with the season, too, and also reminiscing on a Halloween from decades ago when I asked Michelle Adams out on a date and then splashed her in the face with Tink's No. 69 Doe-in-Rut Buck Lure.

Tink's 69 is supposedly the number-one-selling deer lure in America, something I don't doubt because you can buy the stuff just about anywhere in the fall, and it's been that way for as long as I can remember. Part of the reason for its popularity is that it works. Plenty of hunting products are gimmicks, but Tink's 69 is nothing more than urine gathered from a whitetail doe when she's in estrous, bottled, and sold for $10 per ounce. The newer Tink's containers are plastic, but the older ones were amber glass, like beer bottles.

The lure's odor is one of pure, pungent deer sex. I've poured little droplets of it near my stand and then watched bucks go jelly-legged with arousal when they walked downwind of it. When you buy a bottle of Tink's, the packaging even warns not to get the stuff on you before going hunting because horny whitetail bucks could attack. And even if you can avoid being molested by a buck, Tink's 69 is not stuff that you want on your hands because it won't just wash right out. You surely don't want it splashed into your nostrils.

I met Michelle in Mrs. Roby's kindergarten class. We were two of probably 40 kids in the original Dawson Springs class of 2001, but by the time graduation day came, that number had dwindled to 29. Michelle and I always got along, partly because we were both from families of hunters.

Michelle's mom, Mary, was the town librarian, known as "Ms. Mary" to just about everyone. Her dad, Larry, worked at Buckhorn plastics during the day and then on a cattle farm in the evening.

On the rare occasion that he didn't have to work, Larry hunted. Michelle grew up following him to deer camp in the fall and turkey camp in the spring, and sometimes she'd sit with him in his box blind, though she never got to shoot. When Michelle was young, Larry was of the old-school mentality that said girls didn't hunt, even though Michelle asked him to go over and again. When she was 14, she even created a proposal for Larry on a trifold presentation board that outlined all of the reasons why she should be allowed to go hunting, but still, she was allowed to accompany only as an observer.

I didn't know any of that during our grade school years. Michelle just told me that she liked hunting. Once she brought to school a Polaroid of herself posing in camo with a turkey on the family front porch. She told me at the time that she'd killed the bird but revealed later that Larry had actually shot the turkey and that she'd posed with it and was a little pissed off at the time to boot. Still, I was impressed because none of the other girls in our class seemed to care anything about hunting.

One summer day, between our sophomore and junior years of high school, I saw Michelle in Walmart shopping for supplies with Mary, and instead of camo, Michelle was wearing a skintight red shirt. She walked up to me, hair looking golden and soft, and asked if I was looking forward to going back to school, and all of a sudden, yes, I really was.

We had biology together, and early in the fall, we were pairing off with lab partners for the remainder of the year. Michelle asked me right away to be her lab partner, but I told her that I'd probably be working with Robert instead. He was one of my best friends, after all, and had been since the second grade. Although he later became valedictorian of the class, Robert didn't take much of anything seriously in those days, and he was as gifted at bringing out the 16-year-old numbskull in me as he was at academics. Robert could brush school aside and still make straight As. I couldn't.

Bobby Doug, our biology teacher, pulled me aside when he learned of the arrangements being made for his lab. "Brantley, sometimes I'm shocked at what a dumbass you can be for as smart as you are," he said. "Shelly's asking you to be her lab partner, and you'd rather pair up with Robert? I should smack some sense into you. You and Shelly are lab partners, no more discussion. Maybe you'll thank me for it one day."

I told Michelle what Bobby Doug had told me, and she smiled and said, "Don't ever call me Shelly again." Together, we examined the cellular walls of celery under a microscope, spit into petri dishes to grow bacteria, cut up embalmed frogs, and still talked a bit about hunting and fishing on the side. I finally asked her out to a movie on a Saturday, which was Halloween.

But on the Friday night before, there was a costume dance at school. It was a chilly evening, and so I went out bowhunting and didn't plan on going to the dance, but I also didn't shoot a deer, and since I was already dressed in camouflage, I figured I'd drive into town and see how the dance was going. I didn't expect Michelle to be there, but she was the first person I saw, wearing a black and lacy witch's dress. As I walked toward her, Robert and Seymore heckled me from the crowd.

"Let's go drop the tailgate to your truck and sit a while," Seymore said, and I agreed. We turned to walk to the parking lot, and Michelle grabbed my arm and walked with me, as if I were escorting her to a formal while wearing green, knee-high rubber boots.

I lowered the tailgate as planned and shuffled, offering Michelle a place to sit. She smiled and said that she'd stand since she was in a dress and all. Robert and Seymore hopped right on the tailgate, though, watching as if they knew something entertaining could happen at any moment.

"So, did you see any deer?" Michelle asked. I hadn't, and, moreover, I was confused because I didn't know whether to continue with this line of conversation about deer hunting or talk about the embalmed frogs we'd been cutting up or about the date we both knew we had for the next evening. I was stuck in a purgatory of sorts where I needed to impress her but also impress Robert and Seymore, who were sitting on the tailgate, which may as well have been a stadium where they could coax the dumbass out of me with nothing more than smirks.

"No, I didn't see any deer, but it's probably because I didn't put out enough of this stuff," I said, opening my truck door and reaching into the side pocket of my pack, where I had an amber glass bottle of Tink's 69 Doe-in-Rut Buck Lure. "You ever smelled of any Tink's?"

Michelle shook her head no, but she seemed open to the idea. I unscrewed the cap to the bottle and thrust it toward her face just as she leaned in for a sniff. The threads of the bottle hit her right in the nose well before my forward momentum had stopped. Not a lot of deer piss, but plenty enough, splashed her right in the face, and she recoiled as if she'd taken a bite from a live light socket.

"Jesus, Brantley, you are some romantic," Robert said.

Michelle's face was turned downward, and she fanned her nose with both hands.

"Oh my God, I'm sorry!" I said. At least I hadn't called her Shelly. "Don't get that stuff on your dress!"

"Well, why don't you give me the sleeve of your nasty-ass hunting shirt so I can wipe my face!" she yelled. I extended my forearm, and Michelle Adams blew her nose on my sleeve, and it smelled like deer piss, and even Robert was holding his breath for what might come next. It was understood by the other 28 of us in the class of 2001 that Michelle was the type who just might haul off and knock the shit out of you if you got on her bad side, and I thought maybe I'd done just that.

And she did hit me, too, but it was a playful slug right in the shoulder, along with a smile. "Don't bring any of that stuff on our date tomorrow," she said. I remembered that, and when we went to the movies, I left the Tink's in the truck.

ON FACE PAINT
We weren't fooling Mrs. Parker. She knew at a glance that Seymore and I had skipped school that morning to go turkey hunting. I'd washed my face with paper towels in the Dairy Queen sink but had missed some black paint around my ears.

"Your dang war paint got us caught," Seymore whispered.

But a white face glitters like a signaling mirror in the woods. I learned that when I was 10. Dad would hand me a Camo-Compac and tell me to paint up, but I wasn't quite up to the task at that age. He'd inevitably finish the job himself, bracing the back of my head with his left hand so he could apply enough pressure with his right to drive the paint good and deep into my pores. I'd look like a little savage by the time he was done, with only the whites of my eyes showing, but you could stick me in a shadow with some hand-me-down camo and instructions to sit still, and I'd disappear. That was the idea.

One time in the woods, I asked Dad why we didn't just use face masks like everyone else.

"Because they're aggravating, and I can't chew tobacco with them," he said. "Now be quiet and hold still."

I experimented with face masks anyway. But Dad was right. They are aggravating. I tended to take them off while moving between sets during a turkey hunt, which is really the most important time to have your face concealed. I can't hear as well through a mask. One time, while I was drawing my bow on a deer, my kisser button snagged my mask and twisted it around sideways on my head. I might as well have been shooting blindfolded.

I've been painting up since. For years, I was in the minority. A few old-school turkey hunters, like my dad, painted their faces.

And it was the choice of the unruly fringes who shunned Realtree and Mossy Oak in favor of flea-market BDUs. But the turkey hunters on my VHS tapes and in magazines all wore masks.

Then came the Outdoor Channel, and things changed. Face paint is popular again. It's not necessarily used now as camouflage from critters but rather as a fashion complement to large belt buckles and groomed sideburns. Some TV hunters sport face-paint schemes so elaborate that they could pass as a form of artwork from the county fair. The lines are neat, and the symmetry is perfect. For today's trendy camosexual, face paint is a must-have accessory that can even be worn to dinner after a long day's hunt.

But some of us still just want to hide from critters. For that, a proper face painting should be mostly black to help you disappear in the shadows. It should cover your whole mug, or close to it. Apply plenty of pressure and don't skimp. You ought to have enough paint left under your fingernails to touch things up a time or two during the morning. After the hunt, it should stain your whiskers and leave behind a fierce acne infection, even after a good scrubbing. It should ruin decorative bath towels.

I shouldn't judge, though. If you want to wake up an hour early so that you can paint a rendition of the phoenix rising from the ashes across your face, go for it. As long as the phoenix's wings span the breadth of your mandible, it should be sufficient to hide you from a tom turkey. And if your nails are too manicured to contain an adequate amount of excess, I guess you can always carry some extra paint with you in your turkey vest.

At the end of the day, it all still beats wearing a mask. The only real downside is that it's more difficult to skip school to go turkey hunting and fool Mrs. Parker.

THE TURKEY TRUANTS

The alarm on my wristwatch buzzed, signaling the point of no return. It was 7:30, and had Seymore and I stood up and left the woods right then, we'd have gotten back to school just in time for first period.

We'd left the same turkey gobbling on the same ridge the previous two mornings and beaten the tardy bell. But I didn't learn anything in class on either day that was worth leaving a gobbling turkey for.

My own tags were already filled that season, so I was trying to call in a first bird for my best buddy. It was almost as good as carrying a shotgun myself, but it wasn't without its own problems. Seymore was near the top of our class, and damned if he wasn't proud of it. Worse than that, he'd been recognized in elementary school—twice—for yearlong perfect attendance. He never recovered and, in fact, went on to maintain perfect attendance for seven straight school years. A lot of calm and clear April mornings passed him by in that time.

To me, the subject of truancy meant comparatively little during hunting season. I was a good student and didn't make a habit of skipping school, but Dad had been pulling me from class to go hunting since the sixth grade. Once I got my driver's license and a truck of my own, he had to warn me not to let my grades slip simply because it was turkey season.

When my wristwatch sounded, I was yelping on my Lynch Fool Proof box call and sitting against a tree 15 feet behind Seymore, who was looking over the barrel of his 12-gauge. The gobbler was less than 100 yards away—just out of sight beyond a rolling hardwood knob—and roaring at every note. Seymore heard the watch, which I quickly shut off, and he twisted his head, slowly and slightly, in my direction. I assumed he needed to take a calculus test or something and that we'd be leaving, but instead I could tell that he was smiling underneath his face mask. He'd been overtaken by wickedness, and that seven-year perfect-attendance streak was about to be broken. And it looked like the payoff would be carrying a wild turkey out of the woods.

That would've been a great story. But an hour after the decision to skip school was made, the tom's gobbles faded and then finally stopped altogether.

"What do you think happened?" Seymore whispered.

"Pretty sure you scared him off."

"Bull. I think your calling spooked him."

I wanted to hunt the rest of the day, but Seymore said we were leaving. We walked into the front office of our high school decked in full camouflage. My adolescent complexion bore the evidence of hardcore face-paint use. I'd wiped away enough black grease so that Mrs. Parker, who oversaw the front office, could see the zits on my cheeks, but I had missed several black smudges under my ears and on my neck.

"Your dang war paint got us caught," Seymore whispered. "You could've at least washed your face."

"I did, in the Dairy Queen bathroom," I said. "Must've missed some."

"Where have you boys been this morning? Sick, I guess?" Mrs. Parker asked.

"Yes ma'am," I replied. "Both of us, down with the pukes."

"The turkey fever is bad this time of year," she said with a smile and handed a pair of admittance slips across her desk to us. "Now get your butts to class."

That slip, from Wednesday, April 18, 2001, is yellow and faded, and it rides in my wallet behind my hunting license to this day. We checked in at 10:08 a.m., and Mrs. Parker marked it as an excused "unavoidable" absence. Bless her.

I carried the slip for more than 20 years, though somewhat accidentally. I found it in a pile of expired hunting licenses when I swapped wallets a few years after high school and got a chuckle out of it. I decided to keep it. A bunch of hunting licenses—and a few new wallets—have come and gone, but every year in March, when I'm due to buy a new hunting license and begin the year's turkey scouting in earnest, I take that admittance slip out for a look. It's a token of a good memory—but also a reminder of how, despite our best intentions, Seymore and I hadn't hunted spring turkeys together again after April 18, 2001.

The reason is a common enough story of childhood buddies taking different paths, where staying in touch isn't always easy. That was our senior year, and we left for different schools. Seymore settled on the Alabama coast, where he became something of a saltwater fishing bum (in addition to a successful attorney). We managed to go fishing and duck hunting here and there, and we talked a lot about getting back to the turkey woods after that first gobbler. Several springs ago, we realized that 18 years had gotten away, and it scared both of us. There'd been enough talking.

I asked Seymore if he could tear away from work for a few days to go turkey hunting with me in Texas. I knew from the look on his face—overtaken by wickedness—that the answer was yes.

Mesquite and cactus replaced the dogwood petals and redbud blooms of the eastern hardwoods, but South Texas still showed off a rich green that's only seen in the springtime. Hints of light bled into the sky as we debated about the perfect setup in the dark. One of the ranch guides had dropped us off and wished us the best of luck. He said he'd seen some strutters in the area but wasn't sure where they were roosted.

A coyote howl helped narrow the search as a bunch of Rios erupted in shock gobbles 150 yards away. We stuck a couple of decoys in the *sendero* and hustled into the mesquite with only a few more minutes of darkness to conceal our final movements. We cut a good shooting lane through the mesquite thorns and settled in to listen to the new morning. The turkeys gobbled again, and Seymore leaned toward me. "You weren't lying about Rios being noisy," he whispered. "They sound like a bunch of hairdressers."

I choked back a laugh. Eighteen years since we'd last sat down to a turkey together, and some things hadn't changed at all. When we were kids hiking to the Bass Hole, stalking a shagbark hickory tree full of squirrels, or cutting class to hunt turkeys, Seymore and I had always worked well and naturally together in the woods. Anyone who's had more than a couple of hunting buddies knows how important it is to be in step on decision-making, when to keep quiet, and when to laugh.

Rios are fun, and they do gobble a lot. But I have probably messed up on more of them per capita than any other subspecies. "Don't be fooled by all the noise," I said. "They're still turkeys and will screw us over given half a chance."

When the day broke, I made a few clucks and tree yelps, and the gobblers responded instantly. We then kept quiet, but the gobbling only grew more urgent and frequent. When we heard the slap of wings, I made a loud cutt and followed it with a long series of yelps. The toms cut me off—and they'd already covered half the distance.

"I see 'em," Seymore soon whispered. Black forms moved alongside the far edge of the *sendero*, behind a grown-over fence that we hadn't noticed in the dark. For a minute, I was afraid they might hang up behind the old fence—but then I realized I was even more afraid of this hunt ending too quickly. I couldn't tell how many gobblers there were, but I didn't intend to wait for a double. They paused for a bit to drum and display before belting out more gobbles that nearly got the best of us and caused a flinch.

"Man. Haven't heard that sound in a long time," Seymore said. His grip tightened around the shotgun as a longbeard suddenly strutted around the fence and into plain view 25 yards away. The tom spit and drummed, snowball head and red wattles tucked tight to his chest. As he approached our jake decoy, I heard the click of the safety, and the gobbler did, too. He stretched his neck to investigate, and Seymore dropped him with a load of No. 4s.

"All those mornings we put in without getting one," Seymore said. "All those close calls that didn't work out. We skip 18 years, and then it happens in 30 minutes the first time we're back out. Think it's because we're more patient about things now?"

"Could be," I said. "Sometimes I look back at my turkey-hunting self in high school and wonder how I ever stopped calling long enough to shoot one."

After taking photos and cleaning his bird, I mentioned the admittance slip in my pocket. "Mrs. Parker could've turned us in like the delinquents that we were, but she marked that absence as excused," I said. "I guess to her credit, she knew we weren't out selling meth. But do you regret breaking that perfect-attendance streak to keep after a turkey we never even killed?"

Seymore shook his head, seemingly puzzled that I'd even ask. "Never have regretted it."

Fact is, had he maintained that perfect attendance, two best buddies might've never gone turkey hunting in Texas.

OLD TRUSTY

Things were getting serious between Michelle and me, evidenced by the fact that I was going to take her turkey hunting, something she'd always wanted to do. She showed up for an evening hunt with Larry's hand-me-down 12-gauge, a 3-inch 870 Express with a 22-inch barrel and hand-painted camo on the wooden stock. The gun was nicknamed Old Trusty, she said, and if you pointed the barrel of it up into the air and hit the slide release, the action would pop right open, purely from force of gravity; that's how worn in it was.

But neither that nor the fact that the Old Trusty kicked like a battering ram when loaded with Double-X Magnum turkey loads made it unusual to me. I'd been around enough 870s in my day to know that they often got sloppy with age and to hold on tight anytime they were loaded up with anything heavier than a high-brass game load.

Skinning Catfish in Mary's Kitchen

No, what made this gun strange was the Tasco scope mounted on top of it. I'd seen turkey scopes advertised in magazines, but never in the wild. Deep down I didn't believe that anybody would actually need a scope to shoot a turkey, standing still at 30 yards, with a shotgun. But Michelle held up the scoped 870 and said that's what she'd be using because it's what her daddy used. I knew Larry was a hell of a turkey hunter, and besides, had Michelle shown up with a Nerf gun, I'd have exhausted myself trying to call up a gobbler for her.

But Old Trusty worked better than a Nerf gun. Michelle shot her first turkey, a long-spurred gobbler, while hunting with me that afternoon. And the next morning, after a lifetime of only being allowed to tag along as an observer, she went hunting with Larry and killed a gobbler that he called up for her, the first of hundreds of hunts the two of them would go on to enjoy together.

Michelle filled her turkey tags in much the same way for many springs after that. It was almost expected that if she went turkey hunting, she'd get a turkey. Old Trusty patterned with *ferocity*, and you didn't always find turkey guns like that in those days. Gobblers hit with it stayed shot, usually crumpling in a heap with minimal flopping. And Michelle just *never* missed with it.

Turkey hunting ammunition improved rapidly in the early years of our marriage—the timeline is sometimes how I remember important dates—and Old Trusty shot just as well with the new stuff as it did with the old. Michelle loaded up with Winchester Longbeard XR for several seasons before switching over to Tungsten Super Shot, which made Old Trusty even more lethal.

Sometimes when we'd be out hunting, she'd hand me her gun while crossing a creek or fence, and I'd always remark at how heavy the thing was. "You'd save a pound and a half if you'd take the saddle mount and scope off this gun," I'd say. But she liked her scope and said that she didn't miss turkeys but sometimes I did, shooting with a plain bead. And that was true. I didn't miss turkeys often, but I was hunting multiple states each spring by then, and I'd send a bucket of pellets over the top of at least one gobbler at some point during the campaign most years. When it happened, people knew about it because I'd always have myself a little cussing fit in the wake. I've screwed up shots on big bucks and bull elk and bears and all sorts of critters, but to me nothing is more painful than missing a spring gobbler.

Still, I wasn't going to be seen lugging around a shotgun with a scope on it.

But then one morning Michelle's track record with Old Trusty changed. We'd belly crawled to within 25 yards of a gobbler that was hung up on the crest of a white oak ridge. When he spun our way and craned his gaudy head, I heard the safety *pink* on Old Trusty. I figured that turkey was as good as fried nuggets. But instead, Michelle blasted a dogwood sapling 2 feet to the right of the bird, a real shame because the white flowers were pretty on that particular tree. She racked the slide and scrambled to the top of the ridge, looking at the empty ground as if the dead gobbler might appear there if she only paced enough. I didn't say much, but I was secretly delighted because, after all those years, Michelle was due to miss a turkey at least once.

Back home, we set up a target in the yard and soon found that the Tasco scope was giving out, its guts rattled to death by magnum 12-gauge recoil. "It's time you lost this crutch anyway and just start using Old Trusty like a shotgun," I told Michelle. She reluctantly agreed. And she had no problems wielding Old Trusty on ducks and doves and rabbits, racking shells so fast you'd think the old pump was belt-fed. She used it in a layout boat in Maryland to knock down a limit of sea ducks. My buddy Ryan, who had a good set of rabbit dogs at the time, said he'd never seen a woman who could shuck an 870 quite like her.

But something changed when the critters weren't running or flying and instead weighed 21 pounds and stood 4 feet tall and stone still. I'd call spring turkeys up for Michelle, and she'd take the safety off Old Trusty and miss them, not every time but as often as not, when using a straight bead. "I want my scope back," she said.

I got her a Weaver Kaspa turkey scope, a variable-power model with a 30-mm tube that was of much better build than the old Tasco but also about twice the physical size, both longer and heavier. Michelle killed the first gobbler she shot at with it, and her confidence was restored. By that point I'd downsized my own turkey gun even more, toting a featherweight Benelli 20-gauge loaded with TSS most of the time, and so when I'd heft Old Trusty while crossing a fence, I'd find myself in amazement. It truly could've made a useful boat anchor.

One afternoon Michelle and I found ourselves crawling behind a fan toward a big Tennessee gobbler that was strutting with a group of hens in a cut beanfield. We couldn't see the bird, but my buddy Kerry Wix was behind us in the timber, calling to keep it talking so we could keep getting closer. When we finally saw the gobbler and the gobbler saw the fan, it came charging. Michelle leaned out and dropped the bird dead from the prone position with Old Trusty but screamed before racking the slide. The scope had hit her so solidly between the eyes that they both blackened almost instantly. She nursed her face and fought back tears but then told Kerry that I'd decked her in the nose for shooting the gobbler before I could get to it. She walked around with two lingering black eyes for weeks—but that didn't stop her from filling the rest of her turkey tags.

The next spring, down in Texas, Michelle decided to hunt one of her favorite spots alone on the first evening, near a live-oak bottoms where turkeys often roost. To hear her tell the story, she called up a nice Rio Grande gobbler that came in silently. She put the crosshairs on its neck, pulled the trigger, dumped the bird, and went starry from what felt like a right hook between the eyes. Scoped again. She texted to tell me that she had a bird down but left out the detail about the scoping. Her two black eyes made it easy to see what happened, though.

"You're going to detach a retina shooting this gun with that scope," I said and assumed that she'd maybe try practicing some more with a plain bead. Instead, she took the scope off one 870 and put it onto a different one, a 20-gauge that Larry had given her for Christmas years ago but that she'd never used for turkeys. With a Carlson's choke tube and TSS shells, it's almost as lethal as Old Trusty, and the heavy scope and mount help tame the mild 20-gauge recoil even more. She hasn't missed a turkey with it since, though sometimes she still looks at Old Trusty, oiled and retired in the safe, action still slick as ever.

Me, I went all last season shooting gobblers with a plain bead, and I had a great time, until my second-to-last day in Nebraska, when I missed a big Merriam's gobbler clean. Per tradition, I had myself a little cussing fit and admitted—though certainly not aloud—that the bird would've been easy pickings if I'd had a scope on my shotgun.

SKINNING CATFISH IN MARY'S KITCHEN

It can take a while for a potential son-in-law to earn his keep, and it didn't seem like I was off to a great start with Mary, seeing as I'd slapped her in the face with a catfish tail. It sounds worse than it was; the catfish was dead, and I've seen live ones slap harder, and it was an accident besides that. Maybe I shouldn't have been cleaning catfish in Mary's kitchen, but it was her idea, and she was just standing too close while I was using the skinning pliers. A good piece of hide ripped free faster than I meant for it to, and the momentum of it all sent the tail and a rope of guts right into Mary's cheek with a liquid plop. She looked at me, and her eyes narrowed. I recalled a few years earlier when I'd splashed Michelle, Mary's daughter, in the face with deer piss right before our first date. That had turned out okay, but I wasn't sure about this.

I took a moment of silence just to observe, and there was catfish blood and slime running off my knuckles and Mary's cheek both all the while. But I didn't dare speak first. Mary had never scolded me before, but I thought that might be about to change. Instead, she wiped her cheek with her hand and said, "Well, finish that one up." So, I twisted the catfish's head off, and it cracked like smashing a bag of pork rinds. I dropped the severed head into the trash can, split the belly with my pocketknife, sloughed out the rest of the guts, and handed the skinned fiddler to Mary. She walked it to the sink and rinsed it off.

Mary technically wasn't my mother-in-law yet, but Michelle and I had been dating for a few years, and I was trying to earn my keep. We'd all gone catfishing that day—Larry, Mary, Michelle, and I. I'd taken them to one of my favorite bank-fishing spots, in a bay that's choked with lily pads in the summer but that loads up with channel cats and bullheads in the early spring before the pads get too thick.

I've tried worms there but have never done much good on them. It's always a chicken liver bite, and Mary didn't like that we were using up good livers for fish bait when we could've been frying them instead. But she came around because the cats were biting. You could barely bait a hook and set your rod in a forked stick before a catfish would run with it. Larry caught three nice ones in a row, just off a chunk of yellow liver gristle. If you've done any liver fishing at all, then that tells you how hot the bite was because they almost never hit that stuff. We only brought one tub of livers with us and soon, we were out of bait.

We'd parked the truck and hiked a quarter mile into the spot, and we hauled our fish out on a rope stringer, wound around a hickory limb that Larry and I carried on either end. It was a March day, when the woods still looked like winter, but the warm air and daffodils said otherwise. Still, the sun set early, and by the time we were home, it was dark.

I don't remember exactly how the suggestion to clean the fish in the kitchen came up. Catfish skinning is an outside job. But probably, we didn't have a flashlight handy, and Mary's kitchen was well lit. She's always had a pragmatic "solve the problem right in front of you first" type of attitude.

I couldn't have made a bigger mess of her kitchen with a bucket of puke, and to top it off, I slapped her in the face with a dead catfish. I'd say mother-in-law/son-in-law relationships have been severed by less. But that's been 25 years—and many meals and laughs and a few tears ago—in that same kitchen. I bet today, if I had a mess of catfish to clean and it was getting dark with no flashlights handy, Mary would suggest we clean them in the kitchen, and she'd help, too.

She might just stand back a bit while I was working the skinning pliers.

Snakes, Smallmouths, and a Four-Way Wrench

The woman was standing in the Ozark gravel road in a bikini and flip-flops, holding a dead timber rattlesnake around the neck. It was obvious that either she or one of the two dirt-faced kids hovering at her hips had smashed the pit viper's head real good with a rock. Its tail curled slightly in the way a fresh-killed snake's will: enough life to move a bit but not enough to buzz any alarm or thrash out of control. Fresh snake blood oozed across the base of her thumb.

"Saw him lying there in the road!" she beamed. It *was* a dandy snake; 5 feet long, easy, and thick as a man's arm. I doubt she'd have accepted a hundred dollars for it had you offered it up that very moment. "You'ins going down to the river?"

We weren't a half mile from the banks of the Jack's Fork.

"Yes, ma'am," Seymore said, putting his Blazer in park. I was in the front seat next to him, and Robert and Rusty were in the back. We were going bass fishing, and Seymore told the woman so.

"Bass fishing? There's no bass in that river. But I hope you have fun," she said. "Damned if this ain't a nice snake, though." She held it up a little higher so we could all truly admire it and then slowly coiled it into a yellow Dollar General bag. Seymore put the Blazer in drive and continued on down the road.

"Brantley," Robert said as the water came into view, "that local woman says there's no bass in that river."

"She needs to stick to snakes," I said. "The bass are in there."

Dad had been taking my brother, Matt, and me to the Jack's Fork since we were kids, and anytime we fished there, he'd regale us with stories of hard-fighting smallmouth bass. Those sporty fish lived in the slack-water eddies of the clear and flowing river, and they jumped higher and pulled harder than the farm-pond largemouth bass that Matt and I were used to catching.

I'd told Seymore, Robert, and Rusty all about the fishing in the Jack's Fork during the waning days of our high school senior year. It was so good that we ought to catch 100 fish per day between us, and we could do the trip for cheap. A hotel room in Eminence, Missouri, didn't cost more than $40 a night, and we could split it and the gas between the four of us.

We were some distance down the road from the woman and the rattlesnake, following the red rock switchback as it wound toward the river, when the tire blew. Seymore guided the Blazer to the shoulder, what little there was of one, and we all gathered around the flat for a look. At 17 or 18 years old, our collective experience at fixing flat tires was minimal but not absent. Seymore had a jack and a single-socket lug wrench, but it did not fit the lugs on his wheel.

"We're going to have to get a four-way wrench from somewhere," he said. But we were 10 miles from town, broken down on a gravel road, before cell phones existed. Robert treated it all as if it were great news.

"Shoot, me and Brantley will just walk back up there to the snake woman and see if she'll give us a ride into town," he said. "Y'all stay here with the stuff till we get back."

And so, we turned and started walking back up the road, but when we got to the scene of the snake killing, there was nothing left but a spot of dried blood in the gravel. The woman and her kids were gone. We kept walking up the hill, out onto the blacktop and toward Eminence. Robert and I both had been cross-country runners, and so that it was hot and hilly, and we didn't have water, wasn't a huge inconvenience. A couple cars passed us, and we watched them disappear. But when a black pickup approached next, Robert stuck out his thumb. An old man and woman pulled over immediately and asked if we were okay.

"You don't have a four-way lug wrench in there we could borrow, do you?" Robert asked. "We've got a flat tire down the road." The man shook his head no, but said they'd have one at the service station in Eminence and that he'd give us a ride if we wanted because he was headed that way anyhow and it'd be a hell of a long walk. Robert and I climbed inside, crammed shoulder to shoulder against the man and his wife, all across a single bench seat.

"Where you'ins from?" the man asked as we got going. Kentucky, we said, and we're here to fish for smallmouth bass.

"Bass? There's no bass in that river. You should be over on the Ohio fishing for catfish instead of all the way out here," he said. We agreed that being somewhere else was probably a good idea, but we had to fix our tire first regardless.

The man pulled into the parking lot of the service station, let us out, and wished us luck. Eminence is an Ozark town known for its horseback camping and miles of trail riding, and because of that, in the warm months there are flies buzzing just about anywhere you care to go. That day it seemed like most of the flies had converged onto the service station. A horde of them swarmed around the counter when Robert and I walked inside. Behind the counter, and the flies, was a large man in suspenders, sitting on a bar stool with a bowl of Frosted Flakes balanced on his ample gut and a bit of milk dribbling off his chin.

"We're in need of a lug wrench," I said. The man acted as if he didn't hear me at all, even though I was no more than 5 feet away and looking right at him. "Sir?" I said, and he heaved.

"Boys, I made myself a promise about a year ago that if I was eating, I wouldn't do a thing until I got done. Right now, I'm eating Shredded Wheat."

Robert leaned to me and whispered, "Pretty sure those are Frosted Flakes," but he didn't whisper it quietly enough. The man placed his bowl on the counter and waved away a fly that circled over it immediately.

"What'd you say you want?" he asked.

"To borrow a four-way lug wrench. We're out here fishing with a couple of our buddies, and we got a flat tire up the road aways. Didn't have a wrench that would fit."

"I've got a wrench. But I bet you'll just steal it if I give it to you," he said. It had never occurred to me to steal a lug wrench.

"I'll leave you $20 sitting right here, and you can keep it if we don't bring it back," Robert said.

The man shook his head and picked up the bowl of cereal. "I don't believe so."

Robert and I turned and walked back out into the parking lot, no closer to having a lug wrench but agreeing that anyone who confused Frosted Flakes with Shredded Wheat was just the type we didn't want to be in debt to anyhow. Suddenly, a blue Dodge Shadow bounced off the blacktop and rolled to a stop in the service station parking lot. The driver's side window was down, and a small man with a mustache leaned out, brushed away an aggravating fly, and looked at us.

"You'ins look lost," he said. "Need a ride somewhere?"

"Well, what we need is to borrow a four-way lug wrench," I said. "We've got a flat tire off up the road a bit, and didn't have a wrench that'd fit it. Guy in there wouldn't loan us his."

"The guy in there is an asshole," he said. "I don't have a wrench myself, but I bet my neighbor does. His name's Preacher Francis, and he's got every tool in the world. Nice guy, too, being a preacher and all. I'm sure he'd let you borrow a wrench. Jump in, and I'll give you a ride. The front seat's full of junk, so you'll have to get back there."

The Shadow was a two-door car, and so we climbed in behind the passenger seat and arranged ourselves on either side of a cold 12-pack of Busch Lite, which turned out to be the source of our good fortune. The man introduced himself as Eric, and we wouldn't have met him at all had he not run out of beer because he usually didn't come into town otherwise.

We drove back up the road where we'd been walking toward Seymore's disabled Blazer, and Eric quizzed us on why we were there along the way. "Smallmouth bass fishing," I said. "Been coming here since I was a kid, with my family."

"Smallmouth bass, huh. Hell, I didn't even know there was anything in that river but drunks," Eric said, and then he suddenly spun around toward us as if his neck had been on a recoil starter. He was still driving down the road but not looking at it at all, staring at Robert intently instead. "You boys ain't getting into my beer, are you?" he asked.

"No, sir," Robert said. "We didn't even touch it."

Eric turned back around slowly and seemed to focus on the pavement again. "That's good. But hell, reach in and get you one if you want. I think you boys have earned yourselves a cold beer."

Robert seemed to consider it for a minute but thanked him instead and told him that we'd wait. "Suit yourself," he said, and he turned onto a steep hillside drive and pulled the Shadow to a stop in front of a small trailer court. "Just hold on a minute, and I'll knock on the preacher's door for you," he said. Soon, Preacher Francis came outside, with deeply darkened forearms and hands stained black with grease and oil. He smiled, and Robert and I knew we'd found the right man, the sort who wouldn't mistake his cereals and who would let honest folks borrow a tool when they needed one.

"I got plenty of four-way lug wrenches, and you're welcome to use one," he said. Robert offered to leave him some money, but Preacher Francis declined. "Nah, just bring it on back when you're done."

Eric was retrieving his beer from the backseat of the Shadow and gesturing toward another trailer. "That's my place down there. I'm headed inside to have a beer. Keys are in my car. You'ins just take it and get your tire fixed and bring it on back when you're done," he said. Then he nodded at Preacher Francis, who nodded at us, and Robert and I were left standing alone, having gained the use of a four-way lug wrench and a blue Dodge Shadow, too.

Seymore and Rusty looked bewildered when we pulled up in the car, just the two of us. "Where the hell did you get that?" Seymore asked.

"It's Eric's, from up the road," I said. "And this is Preacher Francis's lug wrench. We've got to take them both back when we're done.

"Every person we've met has told us there's no fish in that river," Robert added. "I'm pretty sure Brantley's full of shit, and we should all be out catfishing on the Ohio."

Seymore and Rusty both appeared perplexed, but we all shifted our attention to the tire and in short order had the spare in place and the Blazer going again. Robert and I drove the Shadow back up the road to the trailer court, and Seymore and Rusty followed behind us. Preacher Francis stepped out immediately with a smile and asked if were sure that we were finished with his wrench because we could use it a while longer if not. Eric stepped out, holding a Busch Lite.

"Looks like you'ins got that tire fixed. Want a beer?"

"No, sir, but we do appreciate the help very much," Seymore said and extended his hand to shake Eric's.

"Shit, you don't have to shake my hand, I ain't the president," Eric said. He then nodded at Preacher Francis and walked back toward his trailer.

We pulled to a stop near the gravel shoreline, rigged tackle and split up; two of us waded downstream and two went upstream. We had small, clear-plastic tackle boxes stuffed into swimming trunk pockets, each stocked with Rapala Minnows, Rebel Crawdads, bullet weights, hooks, tubes, green-pumpkin worms, and Salty Craws. It took only a few hours to convince everyone that there were, indeed, bass in the Jack's Fork River—and plenty of them. Every eddy, undercut bank, and slow pool produced vicious strikes. We must've caught 50 fish in a few hours, and a couple of them weighed close to 2 pounds.

"We ought to make this a tradition," Seymore said that night. We were sitting in the breezeway of the motel, split four ways so as to be $10 each. "I mean, getting us all back together for a few days each summer wouldn't be hard."

"Think she ate that snake?" Robert suddenly wondered aloud about the bikini woman we'd met earlier in the day. We all agreed that she'd skinned it and saved the rattles, and after some debate we were mostly satisfied that she'd fried it up and fed it to her kids, too.

We went to bed late and woke up before daylight so as not to miss that early bite. We were there to go smallmouth fishing, after all—and for that, the Jack's Fork River rarely disappoints.

Autumn in August

August, sophomore year at Murray State—I was skinning squirrels in the dorm parking lot when a classmate walked by. I'd seen him around but had never met him. He usually wore a faded camo shirt and boots, though, and so I knew he was a kindred spirit. I yelled at him—"hey!"—and he stopped. "Where you going?" I asked, wiping my blade across my pants. He was carrying a to-go tray from Winslow Cafeteria toward the dormitory where we both lived and where Michelle was a residential adviser.

"Getting closer to a shitter before I even attempt to eat this slop," he said. "Even after two years, my guts still aren't used to it."

"Come over here and help me with these squirrels, then," I said. "I got three good young ones, all out of hickory nut trees. We'll fry them in the community kitchen instead of eating whatever mess you've got there in that tray."

He smiled and introduced himself as Ryan McCafferty. "Shoot," he said. "I'd as soon eat a good young squirrel as a steak." He tossed the dinner tray into my truck bed, where it rode for some time, and opened his own pocketknife. "Were they cutting good?" he asked. "Because I keep a little .410 in my Jeep if you want to go again."

The next morning, a few hours before class, we cut through a thin fog and across a cattle pasture into a 20-acre block of hardwoods. I'd hunted there the last half hour of light the evening before, and I'd have sworn most of the gray squirrels in Kentucky were piled into half a dozen shagbark hickories on the edge of that woodlot. It was already 80 degrees.

"Man, look at the shavings in here," Ryan whispered. He picked up a piece of green hickory husk, freshly chewed by a squirrel. Within a minute, leaves rustled overhead, and a golf ball–sized nut came bombing out of the canopy. A squirrel flashed into view, leaping from one limb to the next. Neither Ryan nor I said a word. He simply eased the little single barrel to his shoulder and thumbed the hammer back with a dull, metallic click. The gun popped, and the squirrel crashed to the ground with a thud. Soon another limb shook overhead, and this time it was my turn to shoot.

With all the hoopla surrounding dove and early goose seasons, you'd think every hunter in the country were finishing up a prison stint on September 1. But the first hunting opportunity in much of the Eastern United States begins weeks before that with squirrel season. It's a great time to hunt. Young gray squirrels born in early summer are freshly weaned and scurrying about in late August. Hickory nuts are beginning to ripen, and squirrels will crowd into the best trees in search of the sweet, new mast.

Finding a good place to hunt is easy. Just about any block of mature hardwood timber will probably have a few hickory nut trees and plenty of squirrels. I prefer to scout in the evenings and hunt in the mornings since August squirrels seem to be most active during the first two hours of daylight. There are a dozen or more hickory species in North America, but two of the most common—and preferred by squirrels—are the shagbark hickory and the pignut. Both have spearpoint-shaped leaves, and the trunk of a shagbark is covered with rough, scaly bark. Learn to identify both types of trees and then simply walk from one to the next, inspecting the ground underneath. If squirrels are feeding in a particular tree, the ground underneath will be littered with pieces of white-and-green hickory nut hull. Set up near such a tree just before shooting light, and action is all but guaranteed.

Ryan and I have squirrel hunted together every season in the 20 years since we graduated from Murray State. Used to be, we'd lean against his Jeep or my pickup in the dark, sipping coffee and watching the morning sky soften on another opening morning. For years, we talked about classes, girls, and beer. Now it's jobs, wives, and kids. But still, every August, when we hear that first hickory nut, one the size of a golf ball, come crashing down to the forest floor, we know it's Autumn again.

Ode to the Boat-Paddle Ruger

I used to think everyone but me hated the boat-paddle Ruger. The M77 Mark II all-weather bolt-action with "Zytel" stock supposedly wasn't accurate, kicked too hard, and looked tacky. It had interchangeable panels on the pistol grip and fore end (most were just black, but some were green, and others were wood grain). The Ruger logo, molded into the face of the buttstock along with the eagle emblem, was like a precursor to the barrel stickers of today but more permanent than an aging tramp stamp. No laser removal therapy would fix the appearance of that stock if you decided you were tired of looking at it.

 The M77 Mark II had a three-position safety and hinged floor plate. It was a rifle of the 1990s, before smartphones, vape pens, and AccuTriggers were things. Back then, factory triggers often broke like rusty trailer latches. Gun writers—who bitched and moaned just as they do today—complained about heavy "lawyer-proof" triggers, and the M77 Mark II had a reputation as one of the worst. Synthetic stocks were relatively new and disliked, too, and the boat paddle stock seemed to especially spit on traditional styling.

 Not that I cared about any of that. I got a boat paddle Ruger in .30-06 on Christmas morning of 1996 or 1997 and thought it was the coolest rifle I'd ever seen. I didn't get a scope for it that morning—Dad would buy that for my birthday a couple months later—but I did swipe three 180-grain Powerpoints from his gun cabinet, and I set a coffee can in the snow maybe 20 yards away. I sighted down the barrel as if it were a shotgun (it didn't have open sights) and blew a massive divot into the snow and mud under the coffee can, sending it spinning into the air. I was able to eyeball the next two shots and punch holes in the coffee can.

 My Ruger wore a 3-9×40 Tasco scope for the next decade, and I used it to shoot lord knows how many whitetails—as well as a bunch of groundhogs, possums, raccoons, coyotes, foxes, and other assorted fauna of Kentucky. I've always had a "guns are tools" mentality, and so my .30-06 was one of just four center-fire rifles that I'd owned in my lifetime when I became hunting editor of *Field & Stream* at age 32. The others were a .22 Hornet, a .308, and an AR. I never knew that I needed anything else.

Maybe some boat-paddle Rugers don't shoot, but mine does. I had a gunsmith buddy work on the trigger some years ago because it *was* heavy. It's still not great by today's standards, but it does break at a crisp 4 pounds. I replaced the scope, too, first with a Nikon Monarch and then a Leupold VX 3i. My rifle has always liked heavy bullets best, and it'll put three 180-grain Nosler Partitions touching at 100 yards if I do my part. Federal's 175-grain Terminal Ascent is a second close favorite, and those old Winchester 180-grain Powerpoints still shoot pretty well. I now own two 6.5 Creedmoors, too, both of which also shoot well but neither of which will outshoot that .30-06 at 100 yards. I've hunted with it in rain and mud and wind and sand and cleaned it once or maybe twice—ever.

Nowadays my "work" hunts usually mean that I'm shooting another manufacturer's new rifle or cartridge, and so I've spent a lot of the past decade chasing big game across the globe with some really good borrowed guns from Browning, Winchester, Springfield, Franchi, Savage, Mossberg, Bergara, and others and in a variety of calibers. When I first took this gig and people asked what kind of rifle I used back home, I'd be a little sheepish in saying it's a decades-old Ruger .30-06—and I'm not sure I've ever told anyone in the "industry" that it's a bolt-paddle model. In this age of hybrid target/hunting rifles, new calibers, and long-range everything, my old Ruger is unimpressive.

Then again, it still works. Last March I was pig hunting in Texas, and Ryan called at about sunset, just as a sounder of sows and shoats stepped into sight. I answered him, put him on speakerphone, and said, "Be quiet and listen." The shooting started, and I killed three pigs in three quick shots. "That sounded like that Ruger," Ryan said, though he was just assuming because he's hunted with me more than most.

"Hell yeah, it was," I said. We talked for a bit, and shortly after we hung up, I killed two more pigs. "Fruitful" is a good word for the success I've had with that rifle, and that's why I reach for it over and again.

Ryan used to own a boat-paddle Ruger, too—in .270—but like many others he sold it years ago because it kicked so hard. But he was the first to tell me that, in a delicious and ironic twist, the boat paddles have become expensive collector's items. "Man, they're bringing a fortune on Gunbroker," he said. "I guess I shouldn't have sold mine."

I checked, and sure enough, the rifles are bringing $1,500+ right now—about three times what Dad paid for mine back in the 1990s. Reading some rifle forums, and it seems a lot of people don't understand the demand for such a hideous, inaccurate rifle that was discontinued long ago, especially when there are so many much better rifles out there today.

Well, to hell with what they think. Fifteen hundred won't touch mine.

Paid to Fish

I'd cross the wooden plank bridge at around 7:15 most mornings, and the bass would usually be there when I did, waiting in the still pool underneath the bridge for a minnow or a crawdad to drift by. I guessed her at about 18 inches long and maybe 3 pounds, a hell of a creek fish and as forbidden as the famous apple.

That bridge crossed the creek between the No. 4 tee box and green on the golf course at Pennyrile Forest State Park. I was a golf maintenance man, and my job was to set the cups and flags each morning after clocking in, rake the sand traps, and mow the driving range and the rough along the edges of the fairways, with a Ford tractor and a Jacobsen Blitzer reel mower.

For the last couple hours of each day, at least if it was hot, all of us maintenance men drove our golf carts to assigned greens, coupled long hoses into underground spigots, and hand watered the bent-grass greens and collars. All of the greens had sprinkler systems, but Ricky, the course superintendent, didn't think the sprinklers were as effective as hand watering for keeping the greens looking nice.

Golf maintenance was a good job for a college student who didn't mind getting up early and mowing grass and sweating and sitting on tractors. That was the only type of job I'd ever had. I never played a single round of golf—and still never have—but I was outside, and most mornings there'd be deer to look at in the fairways and sometimes a gobbler strutting on a green. And of course, there were bass in the water hazards, always tempting me to bring a fishing rod to work, even though fishing wasn't allowed on the golf course and bass fishing sure isn't what I was being paid to do on the maintenance staff.

I clocked in one damp, cloudy morning, and Ricky told me to go ahead and set the cups, even though he didn't expect there to be many golfers that day. Rainy days were for puttering around the maintenance shop; we didn't mow for fear of rutting up the course, and God-given rain was the only thing better for bent-grass greens than hand watering with a hose.

I jumped in my cart, but on my way out of the parking lot of the maintenance shop, I eyed the spinning rod that I'd left in my truck from fishing a watershed lake the evening before. I had a 4-inch weightless trick worm tied to it, pumpkinseed with a red tail. I grabbed the rod and stashed it in my cart, hoping Ricky didn't see it.

The golf carts that the maintenance staff used were all gas-operated, and most were slow, especially those given to the summer help. Bobby Clark, the full-time shop mechanic, had disabled the governor on his cart, and it would sing, but mine lagged as if bound by molasses in the axle if I floored the throttle. As such, it seemed like I'd never make it to the No. 4 bridge. It was raining when I did get there, and I looked around and didn't see any witnesses, golfers or otherwise. I felt dirty as a drug dealer, fishing on the clock, but I promised myself I'd take only a few casts and just that one time. The trick worm barely hit the water's surface before the bass engulfed it. The line grew taut, swimming to the side as I turned the reel handle a couple times to take up the remaining slack and set the hook.

The bass thrashed and jumped, and I pulled it to the edge of the water, lipped it, and admired it for a moment. "Man, here I am getting paid to go fishing," I remember thinking to myself and figuring that was as close as I'd ever get to such a job. I released the bass and got back on my cart, satisfied, and set the rest of the cups.

Ricky, Bobby Clark, and the rest of the maintenance crew were standing in the shop, watching it rain, when I pulled back up. Ricky watched me put the spinning rod back in my truck. "You catch that big bass that's been hanging under the bridge there at 4?" he asked. My face flushed, but I smiled and nodded.

"Yeah, I couldn't stand it anymore. I let him go, though, he's fine, probably sitting in the same spot already."

"Doesn't hurt to take a cast every now and then when no golfers are watching," he said. He'd pulled his truck to the edge of the open bays of the maintenance shop, dropped the tailgate, and had charcoal smoking in a small grill. He'd treat his staff to a good grilled burger sometimes, on a day when it was raining and things were slow.

There were golf course volunteers at Pennyrile, mostly retired men who loved to golf and would help us set cups and water greens in exchange for a discount on their greens fees. Johnny Peroddy was the volunteer on duty that day, but since I'd already set the pins and since it was pouring down rain, he was standing in the shop with us, watching Ricky's charcoal.

"Brantley, what are you studying down there at Murray State?" he asked me. "Game warden?"

"I'm in journalism school actually and minoring in creative writing."

Johnny looked at me as if I'd told him I was studying French theater and becoming a vegan, too.

"Huh. Not what I pictured you doing. So, you wanting to be a newspaper reporter?"

"No, I want to write articles for hunting and fishing magazines," I said.

Johnny paused for a moment as if he'd been stricken with déjà vu or had remembered something that had been told to him years ago but that he'd forgotten everywhere except deep in his subconscious.

"No shit. You know, I've got a buddy, and his brother-in-law, I think it's his brother-in-law, is the editor for *Field & Stream* or *Outdoor Life* or something. I'll put in a good word for you," he said.

I nodded. "Thank you. That would be cool."

Ricky kept working on his charcoal, and then he took some pre-patted burgers out of his cooler.

That fall, after classes started back at Murray State, I got a call from the executive editor of *Outdoor Life*, who'd heard about me from his brother-in-law—I think it was his brother-in-law—who'd heard about me from his friend, Johnny. The editor asked if I'd be interested in doing a summer internship. And I was. The downside was that I had to leave the golf course, which was a good place to work, especially on those cloudy, damp days, when the golfers weren't playing but the bass were biting and the charcoal was going.

BAKER'S THUMB

I haven't shot in a pistol competition since the day Logan Baker cut off most of his thumb.

We were buddies in college, and we both had the range bug, spending money we didn't have on ammo that was destined to be burned on cow turds and Clorox bottles. Jay, the owner of the little gun shop we frequented, would pass us more boxes of FMJ ammo, and we'd give him our cash. Jay fancied himself a tactical guru, but he had a hell of a gut, and he manned his gun counter from a roller stool surrounded by an ever-present cloud of Marlboro smoke.

But one Friday he told us about an open IDPA match at his gun club. It sounded like fun. We'd need even more ammo than usual, he said, and double magazine pouches for our belts, too. Baker went ahead and bought a new holster.

Gunfighting with cardboard targets while a timer's running is fun. Baker and I had similar scores by the end of the match, and neither of us were dead last. There was an old man with a revolver and a bad hip, and we both beat him pretty good. But add in the match fees, and it was all getting expensive.

"You know, we could get us a timer and just make our own targets," Baker said on the drive back. "It'd be cheaper than driving down there and paying to shoot."

"I'd have go by Jay's for more ammo before we do that," I said. "I wanted to keep at least a full magazine, but I couldn't help myself. I shot up every bullet I had. Plus, I've got class this afternoon."

But you couldn't stop Baker once he was stricken with a good idea. He'd skip class and put the expenses on a credit card if he believed a project to be important, and at that particular moment nothing in the entire world was more important than the two of us doing some more timed pistol shooting. Baker was living in a rental house and had a decent supply of tools and some scrap lumber in the corner, and so he decided to begin making the targets immediately. I promised to come right back to help him once I'd gone to class and bought some more ammunition.

But Baker's garage was empty when I returned. There was a Styrofoam bow target—the $13 kind used at summer camps everywhere—some chunked up 2-by-4s, a circular saw, and a bloody piece of notebook paper that said,

Brantley: At hospital. Cut my thumb off. Also, you left your pistol in my car. —LB

For all the tools and wood in Baker's rental-home garage, there were no sawhorses, and sawhorses are surprisingly expensive. But the bow target was sitting right there, and so was the circular saw, and so Baker had been buzzing through weathered 2-by-4s, making them into 3-foot target stakes, and using the bow target to balance everything. The saw had bucked a bit and gotten just squirrely enough to whir into the web of Baker's off hand and deep into the bone of his thumb.

Baker was drugged up and belligerent when I got to the hospital, mostly because the doctor had wanted to catch the end of a ball game before sewing his thumb back on. But his hand was wrapped, and all signs pointed to things healing mostly correctly. I shuffled around for a minute, trying to think of something sensitive to say before Baker finally relieved me. "You asshole," he slurred. "I know why you're here. My keys are in my pants pocket. Go on out there and get your gun out of my car."

A week later, we went shooting, but down at the creek and at Clorox bottles. Baker got pretty good at blasting those bottles with one hand. It hadn't cost us any entry fees, and we managed to have fun on a 50-round budget.

I told the whole story several years later, during Baker's wedding reception, where I was best man. I had to wear a tux, which I didn't especially like, but Baker had sacrificed his own thumb for our friendship. Dressing up before getting his new family to laugh about it was the least I could do.

With a Fish Fry at the End

On my last night as a student at Murray State and just days before Michelle and I got married, Seymore and I set the dormitory community kitchen on fire.

It was mid-May, and Seymore, who'd just finished up at the University of Louisville, had driven in to go bluegill fishing with me. By sunset, we had 40 big bream on ice. Finals were over, so the dorm was mostly vacant, save for a few holdouts like me, and the squad of residential advisers, whom everyone called RAs.

The RAs didn't really *advise* on anything but instead assumed the role of dormitory law enforcement, ensuring that the college students under their supervision never engaged in things like drinking alcohol or playing loud music and also that they paid the fees owed to the university on time. It was a corrupt system, and Michelle was as crooked as any of them. She'd written me up only a few days earlier because I'd thrown away a mattress pad supplied by Murray State that very well could've been a biohazard. "I wasn't sleeping on that damn thing," I told her. "It was disgusting, stained with who knows what. Plus, we're getting married in like a week. Can't you cut me a break?"

"No," she said. "Here's your citation."

The $35 I'd been forced to pay Murray State for a crusty mattress pad was fresh on my mind when Seymore and I pulled into the parking lot with bream to clean. We'd already bought cornmeal, frozen french fries, and vegetable oil.

"What we ought to do," Seymore said as he honed his fillet knife against a steel, "is have us a little whiskey while we cut up these fish." I agreed.

Michelle was working the front desk when I walked in, and so I kissed her on the cheek. "We having fried fish for dinner?" she asked.

"Yep, we did pretty good, have 40 bluegill on ice. I'm headed up to the room now to get some whiskey to drink while we clean them."

"Will Brantley, do *not* let me see you drinking whiskey on school property! It's against the rules!"

"Okay. I will not let you see it."

I swaddled a two-thirds bottle of Early Times in a hand towel as if it were a newborn baby and carried it and two coffee cups past the front desk with a glaring Michelle and out to the parking lot, where Seymore was already filleting fish on his tailgate. We only needed an hour to finish them and a good bit of the whiskey both.

The community kitchen was just down the hall from Michelle's front-desk post. We had a single 12-inch, cast-iron skillet for frying 80 fillets and 2 pounds of fries. "Reckon we'll eat all of this?" Seymore asked.

"Hot oil always attracts a crowd down here," I said. "We'll run out of fish, feeding people we've never met."

As the pile of fillets grew on a paper towel–lined cookie sheet, Seymore and I began sipping the rest of the whiskey right off the threads because there didn't seem to be enough time to pour it into the coffee cups first. "Man," I said, balancing an arm against the counter and squinting at the skillet. "We ought to finish dinner before I have any more of that."

Seymore shook a few of the frozen fries into the grease, where they popped and sizzled. "Hell, we'll never finish at that pace. Fill that skillet up!" I said, wrenching the bag from his hands and ripping it open. The remainder of the fries rolled into the skillet in a frozen clump. Oil sloshed onto the burner, and the stove erupted into a 3-foot ball of flame.

Seymore, ever the quick thinker, grabbed the open bag of cornmeal and dumped it onto the element as I shut off the burner. The meal extinguished the flame but was seared immediately into a black sludge that sent smoke billowing through the dorm. The fire alarm rang; we could hear students scrambling and screaming down the stairway and through the smoke.

Michelle appeared before us in the doorway of the kitchen, trembling with anger, like a little specter in the smoke. "The fire department is on its way," she said.

"Well, the fire is already out!" I said defiantly. The stove was still billowing smoke as if hit by a meteorite. Seymore grabbed the whiskey bottle and had himself a little nip, right in front of her. Michelle tightened her gaze at the two of us.

"I mean, what's it really hurt at this point?" he asked, wiping his upper lip. "Besides that, I don't go to school here, and, Michelle, you're not the boss of me!" The fire truck pulled right up to the front door, lights flashing and siren wailing. Six uniformed men marched inside, and Michelle happily directed them toward us.

Two industrial fans were needed to purge all the smoke from the building, and far as I know, the place still smells burned.

"Damned if those firemen didn't eat every fillet of fish we had," Seymore said after they left. Sure enough, only a few golden crumbs and a glob of charred fries remained. We had to order pizza to offset the whiskey, but before it got there we decided to go to the parking lot, where Seymore had a cooler of beer stashed in his truck. We finished a few cans of that and then lined the empties up like targets across the pavement so as to have a casting contest. Seymore tied a heavy bass jig to his flipping stick, and we passed it back and forth.

"I reckon I'm going to law school," he said, "and you're going to be the Great Outdoor Writer, who still can't cast as good as I can, even if it is part of your job." *Ping*. He plunked over an empty can with a perfect pitch. "Dead soldier right there, son!"

Five days later, in a little church in Dawson Springs, Michelle and I said our marriage vows. Seymore was among the groomsmen, wearing a camo vest and high-balling on a double-reed duck call during the recessional.

Chapter Three
Birds, Lions, Flatheads, and Murder

Out of the Smoke

They could've been carrier pigeons, flying through the smoke and pops of gunfire on some century-ago battlefield to relay an important message. But they were just doves, hellbent on eating popcorn. Ryan McCafferty and I knelt in the shadow of a tobacco barn that had wisps of smoke curling from its rafters, waiting to shoot at the birds when they popped over the roof and into sight, only a little higher than the barn itself. Most of them had already set their wings and were gliding into the picked field by the time we saw them. As doves go, it was easy shooting.

Tobacco barns, where some varieties of tobacco (collectively called dark-fire) leaves are cured by smoke prior to being sold, are still common in western Kentucky if few other places. Every year, people out driving the countryside (mostly people from town) call fire departments to report barns that are apparently on fire. The calls happen so frequently, in fact, that local news outlets give public service announcements, starting in August, to remind folks that barns billowing smoke are part of a perfectly normal, regional farming practice.

For a few glorious weeks in the early fall, the barns make the countryside smell like a smoking pipe. Michelle says the smell reminds her of her grandfather, who grew a few acres of his own tobacco and was known to pluck leaves from the rafters as it was curing and make his own twists, which he kept in a shirt pocket. When she was just a little girl, the old man would hire Michelle to weed his garden (all 3 acres of it) and then pay her a full dollar wage at the end of the day. Then they'd sit on the porch in the evenings, and he'd hand her his twist so she could bite off a plug and have a little chew. To this day she can spit tobacco juice halfway across the yard and hit a stray dog if so inclined, but she would be embarrassed if anyone knew that.

For me, the dark-fire smell is one of squirrel season and teal season and dove fields, at a time of year when fall is about to begin, guaranteed. At the same time that farmers are curing tobacco in the barns, they're broadcasting wheat on the dirt fields where it was just cut. Silage is being chopped, and the first cornfields are being shelled. Strips are mowed in plots of sunflowers and millet. The harvest creates a smorgasbord for mourning doves, and the birds arrive here by the thousands on the heels of the tiniest cold fronts. Unlike scouting for teal, which is particular, anyone with sense enough to walk outside and look up at a power line can tell if a push of doves has come through or not.

Of course, there's a difference in seeing scattered birds on the power lines and having permission to hunt a field where a thousand of them have been feeding every day. That's the other reality of this time of year. You'll know if you've been a good friend for the past 11 months—or at least if you're owed favors—because formal dove shoots are happening and either the phone will ring with your invitation or it won't. It is poor form to call and invite yourself to a shoot (or really even hint about it). But the truth is, the mediocre corners of dove fields are filled every fall in just such a shameless way. This time of year is so sacred, so short-lived, that sometimes you do what's required to get out there.

Having an affable buddy like Ryan helps. I don't think I've gone without a spot to shoot at doves in the 20-plus years that I've known him. A few years ago, we set up in a 20-acre field of marijuana—or at least, that's what the industrial hemp plants looked like and smelled like to me and apparently to others, too, since there were public service announcements that fall, in addition to the tobacco ones, reminding folks that the plants in the hemp fields didn't have enough THC to make stealing and smoking them worthwhile. But the doves liked the seeds, and we made a lot of "high flyer" jokes about the spot. The hemp craze, at least around here, was short-lived compared to tobacco.

To this day, that popcorn field we hunted back in college ranks near the top of my list for all-time favorite dove shoots. I was a journalism major then, trying to become an outdoors writer, and I knew a lot of communications majors and English professors but nobody useful as far as hunting spots were concerned. But Ryan was an ag major and also good at fixing things. As I remember the story, he was oil stained and knuckle busted after working on a local farmer's ailing tractor. When he got done, he looked the farmer in the eye and said, "If you don't mind, me and my buddy are going to come back in the morning and kill those doves lighting in your popcorn field across the road, next to the tobacco barn."

This would not be a formal shoot. Most of those begin around noon, partly to allow for socializing and eating and partly because most of those shoots are on opening day, when legal hours don't begin until 11 a.m. Ryan and I have never been overwhelmed with invitations to anything formal, dove shoot or otherwise. But that was okay because we actually enjoyed hunting later in the season better, when you could start shooting 30 minutes before sunrise.

The best dove hunting, like the best hunting for most things, is right at daybreak, especially if you're set up on a good food source. We began that morning hiding in a fencerow on the far side of the popcorn field. We fired a shot or two but noticed several waves of doves roll over the top of the tobacco barn and then spill out into the popcorn stubble, like droplets of water from a heaved bucket. "I think we might ought to move over there," Ryan said, and so we did, flushing the birds out of the field as we walked but knowing they'd come right back. And they did.

Neither of us shot a limit that day, but we did get plenty to put on a charcoal grill outside the dormitory that night. It was a good meal, especially at that time of year, when tobacco is in the air and you know fall is guaranteed.

The Bird Hunter's Club

It was late August when I knocked on the old man's door, down in Graves County, a row-crop county in southwest Kentucky where people weren't suspicious of a stranger at the door. The old man shook my hand as I introduced myself and then asked about bowhunting behind his house.

"My grandsons hunt back there, otherwise I'd let you," he said. And then, in the way an old man often will, he added his second hand to the shake and narrowed his eyes under gray brows. "Say your name's Brantley? Are you any relation to the Brantley from around Dawson Springs? Big bird hunter? Lawyer, I think?"

I nodded and told him, yes, that's my dad. But he doesn't have bird dogs anymore.

"Son," the old man said, "your daddy and his buddy used to come down here and kill a lot of birds, more than anybody else. I had bird dogs back then, too, but I just wasted my time going to a farm after they'd hunted it. Some of the old bird hunters around here still talk about them."

That buddy of Dad's would've been Donald Stevens, and even though I was just a toddler in the days the old man was referring to, I know what he was saying is true. Mention quail hunting these days, and a portrait of a genteel sportsman following groomed setters with an expensive over/under might come to mind. But it wasn't always like that.

Dad and Donald, like many outdoorsmen in the years before the whitetail deer craze, were bird hunters, and "bird" meant quail. They wore faded flannel and army surplus wool that seemed to grab at cockleburs from three steps away. Donald carried a Browning A-500 covered in camo tape, which was also his turkey gun in the spring. For a while, Dad carried a 16-gauge 870 Wingmaster, but later he switched to a Browning B-80.

The pair of them hunted virtually every day of the season for years. Dad's small-town practice was budding at the time, but during bird season he routinely showed up to work late, wearing his hunting clothes, or early, with a box of whining dogs in the bed of his truck.

Donald worked third shift at the coal mines and, after having worked all night, would meet Dad to hunt all day. "I'd see him pull into the driveway in his old car right after sunup," Dad said. "He'd step out and stretch and nearly fall asleep right there, still in his work clothes from the night before. The trunk latch didn't work right on that car, so Donald kept a screwdriver with him to open it. He'd fiddle with the lock a while, and the trunk would suddenly pop open. It'd be cold, so this ball of steam would roll out. A pile of bird dogs would bound out of the steam and bark and yip and find spots to shit in the yard. Donald would get his hunting clothes, drag himself inside, and lay down on the couch. He'd lay there a while, Mama would fix him breakfast, and then we'd go hunt."

Dad was a good wing shot, but Donald was a phenom. Guns had to be plugged to hold a maximum of three shells, but legend had it that Donald kept an extra shell between his index and middle fingers when approaching a dog on point and often pulled off four shots that all killed birds, on the rise. Dad said that Donald was the only person he'd ever seen who purposely waited until two birds lined up in flight to kill them both. And, when the shooting was done, Donald knew where all his birds had fallen—as well as those of whoever else was shooting.

"Hunting alongside Donald Stevens was the only reason I quit shooting a pump and bought my first automatic," Dad told me.

After my younger brother, Matt, was born and I got big enough to follow Dad around the house and bug him with questions but not quite big enough to follow him in the field, Dad gave his bird dogs to Donald and put his shotgun in the cabinet, at least for a while. He told Mom, "I won't force the boys to play sports they don't want to play or make them go hunting or fishing if they don't want to go—except for one thing. They will shoot at a pointed bird at least once in their lives."

He held to his word. I shot my first quail when I was maybe 12, over an ancient and hardheaded liver-and-white pointer that Donald loaned to Dad for the afternoon. That dog refused to listen to whistles, commands, or even the harshest cussing, but she was rock solid on point. We'd lost her for nearly an hour that afternoon on Joe and Dub's farm before finally catching a glimpse of her white, locked-up frame next to a blackberry briar thicket. Dad told me to step in, stay even with him, and be ready. We did, and a dozen quail boiled out of the briars right at our feet. I shot one time in their general direction, and a bird fell. Dad killed two. I was hooked.

Two years later, that pointer was still in Dad's pen, along with a couple newer dogs. After a decade-long hiatus, Dad was bird hunting again, and I was almost always with him. We hunted with Donald a lot, as well as Bobby Abbott, another close family friend. I followed them and their dogs for miles on weekends and sometimes on weekdays if the weather seemed better for bird hunting than going to school. We'd often begin the days by listening for quail whistling at daylight and then turning out the dogs. By lunch, the first heat of dogs would be worn out, and we'd need a new farm to hunt, so we'd box them up, drive to another place, and then turn another brace of dogs loose.

We had our favorite dogs and our backups. None of them were field-trial dogs, but most were acceptable to top-notch meat dogs. Some could find birds but wouldn't honor another dog's point; others were slow but fantastic on dead birds. And of course, there were always pups in progress that would blunder into a covey and make everyone mad. So, we'd try to stagger them according to their strengths—a good dog or two and a backup in the morning and a similar arrangement that afternoon. Hunting the pups with the good dogs was the best way to train them.

I rode in the back seats of old four-wheel-drives while the men explored side roads they'd hunted years earlier. We'd pull up to a dilapidated farmhouse, and they'd squabble back and forth on whether the old woman who'd lived there 10 years ago had let them hunt, which of them had asked her back then, and whom she would be more likely to remember. One of them would eventually step out and knock on the door, and a new owner, usually some relative of the previous old woman, would appear, chat for a while, and, occasionally, give us permission to hunt.

"There used to never be a problem with just pulling over and turning the dogs out for a couple hours at about any little farm you wanted," Dad said. "All those little farms had birds, too. Their fencerows were grown up between the bean fields, and you didn't see fescue growing everywhere."

"Never be a problem" was partly nostalgic generalization, of course. The occasional landowner would actually take real exception to hunting without permission. A couple times a season, the story of the old woman who pulled a long-barreled revolver on Dad and Donald would come up.

"We didn't think anybody lived in that old place," Dad said. "Hell, you could see between the boards in the house, and I don't even think there were windows to it. We'd hunted it before and killed some birds and never seen anyone. So, we pulled over and turned the dogs out, and when we crossed the yard, this old woman was standing at a clothesline, wearing one of those pilot's caps with the ear covers on them. She had tobacco spit dribbling down the corners of her jaws, and when she saw us, I heard her mumble something.

"I looked at Donald, and before I could say anything, she pulled this long-barreled pistol out of her dress pocket, pointed it at us, and yelled, 'I said come here! People don't pay me much attention because they think I'm crazy. Then I get ol' Bessy out, and they listen better.'"

Donald, a quieter guy than Dad, would often chime in here. I knew the ending to the story but loved to hear it when both of them told it together, particularly when they'd imitate the old woman's shrill voice.

"She had that gun waving around, and I believed her that people thought she was crazy. Your daddy started telling her that we didn't mean any harm, and if she wouldn't kill us, we promised we'd never be back. But turns out, she didn't mind for us hunting. She just wanted us to ask first. We shot a limit of birds that day."

There were countless other stories, and so many of them ended with Dad and Donald "shooting a limit of birds that day." They hunted Graves County a lot, so the old man's reference could've been to any number of trips.

There was lots of reminiscing about the good old days, of course, and then that would lead to commentary about how much things had changed. When those conversations began, there seemed to be more ominous things in the air that remained unsaid. Posted and Leased signs were common sights at once-favored farms. You didn't see coveys of birds running across the road anymore. Finding a couple of coveys in a day's time was about the best you could hope for, and there were many days when you didn't find anything. The bird hunter's club was dying, and they knew it.

I mostly quit bird hunting after a few years once I got my driver's license. I'd gotten tired of all the walking and carrying shotguns that I never got to fire, so I took up duck hunting. Dad kept on bird hunting, though, even after I left home for college. I'd always ask him how the hunting had been when I'd call home during bird season, but the reports were rarely good. Just no birds and nowhere to hunt them anymore, he'd say. Finally, he began giving his dogs away, except for one, a little female setter that retired on a cushion, right at the foot of Dad's bed.

Lil's Last Hunt

I'm just old enough to have seen the end of Southern quail hunting. Yeah, there are still some plantations where a man can shoot at a pointed bobwhite, but bird hunting the way Dad did it was already fading fast when I was born. He saw it coming. The fescue, the coyotes, the clean fencerows, and deer leases seemed to be conspiring against quail hunters. I was in middle school and already beginning to lose interest in the long walks with no points when Dad got his last two puppies.

Sal was a lemon-and-white English pointer representative of the breed: hard-charging with a good nose and an indifference to affection. Lil was a small Llewellyn setter. She didn't have Sal's raw drive, but her nose was good enough. Better than that, she wanted to please. While Sal hunted with you, Lil hunted for you. Once, when she was young, Dad corrected her for marking a quail's breast with a tooth. Her feelings were so hurt that from then on, she would only delicately pick a dead bird up to show it to you and then place it back on the ground.

Sometimes after school, I'd take Lil hunting by myself. There were a few coveys within walking distance of the house, and because she worked close and would always come to me, I never worried about losing her. Killing a single bird was a good day.

Hunting with both dogs was reserved for the weekends and Christmas break, when I'd ride in the truck with Dad and his buddies for an hour or more to the last of their best places—farms that, without fail, used to be better. We shot quail, and my image of real bird hunters was formed. These guys cussed and argued. They didn't carry over/unders because two shells made it tough to kill three birds on the rise.

Such a feat seemed impossible to me anyway, fast as flushing coveys evaporated into the brush. I'd usually empty my gun, but the best I'd ever managed was a lucky double with a single shot. "Pick one bird and then the next," Dad would say. "And always be ready for the late one."

But with each season, the miles between points increased. Sal, with the yellow face, was the first to show gray on her muzzle. I got my driver's license, and my buddies and I discovered boats and duck decoys. I stopped quail hunting with the old men.

Dad would often tease me and ask, "Why would anyone get up that early to shoot a greasy duck when they could hunt birds?" But he knew.

Dad gave Sal away to his buddy Donald Stevens when I went to college. Lil retired indoors. After a life in a kennel, she'd taken to sleeping on a cushion at the foot of my parents' bed. One fall weekend when I was home from school, Matt Seymore called to say he'd flushed a covey of quail while bowhunting his grandmother's farm. The place was only 70 acres, with a small beanfield and dense blackberry thickets, a property reminiscent of another time.

Seymore, Michelle, and I decided to hunt the birds with Lil, who rode in the bucket back seat of my truck to get there. She probably hadn't been hunted in two years, but when we parked, she bounced right of the truck toward a blackberry patch and was on point by the time our guns were loaded. When the covey flushed, the shooting was easier than I remembered. I knocked down two. We picked up a couple of the singles and moved on.

We found three coveys, all told, in two and a half hours. The last boiled from a stand of volunteer kobe lespedeza, right at Lil's nose. My first two birds fell in plumes of tawny feathers. A late bird rose at the shots, and as it banked left to right, I downed it with my final shell. I'd killed three on the rise.

Lil wouldn't bring the birds to us; that scar from her youth ran deep. So, we scrambled to retrieve them, laughing as she found each one, picked it up, and then placed it gently back onto the ground. Our vests were brimming. It was the best day of bird hunting I've ever seen.

It was also the last for Lil and me both. I haven't quail hunted since, and Lil spent her final months mostly curled up on her warm cushion, almost seeming to smile as she slept. One morning, she just stayed asleep. To truly understand the "good old days," you need to have lived them if only for an afternoon. For a couple of hours in the sunset of her life, Lil and I did just that.

Handfishing on the Yeah-Zoo River

At 1:00 a.m., I knocked on the door of our single-bedroom apartment hard enough to wake Michelle and probably some neighbors, too. The walls were thin at that complex where we lived, and I hated to make so much noise, but I needed her to unlock the door. She did, with a .44 Special revolver in her right hand, held down at her side. She wanted to know why I was making such a racket in the hallway at that hour. My hands were so cut and skinned from the jaws of a flathead catfish, I explained, that I couldn't stand to stick them into my pocket to get my keys. I showed her my knuckles, which were peeled, blistered, and oozing pus.

"Heaven help," she said. "That's from a fish bite?"

"Yes," I said. "And I think our lives are about to change."

It was 2005, and we'd been married for a few weeks. I was working for FLW Outdoors at the time, a tournament fishing organization, as an associate editor and communications specialist. My day mostly involved writing press releases about fishing competitions but sometimes articles for their in-house magazine as well. It was for that magazine that I pitched the idea of going catfish noodling and writing about the experience in first person.

Today, if you Google "catfish noodling," you'll get pages of online article and video results about it. A fair bit of that stuff has my name on it, but most of the more recent, popular content has been hosted by Instagram and YouTube influencers like Hannah Barron. But 2005 was years before Instagram existed, and noodling was more obscure then. Most of the coverage I'd seen about it had been done by Wade Bourne, a Tennessee outdoor writer who wrote for *Outdoor Life* and hosted a television show, *Southern Outdoors*.

I'd met Wade, briefly, during my internship at *Outdoor Life*, and so I e-mailed him to ask if he had any leads on a catfish noodling guide. He called me almost right away and shared a phone number for a contact that he had in Mississippi, a guy named Bob who fished on the Yazoo, Tallahatchie, and Yalobusha rivers.

"Bob's not a guide, but he would probably take you," Wade said. "But be forewarned. He's rough around the edges. Sort of what you'd expect from somebody who wrestles giant catfish with his hands."

Bob answered right away when I called him. I told him my name and that I was friends with Wade Bourne and a magazine writer myself and that I wanted to go noodling and not just to watch. "It's handfishing. Only Yankees call it noodling," he said. "Come on. We're gonna go, and I don't give a damn who goes with us. Lots of people think they want to try it till it's time to get in that river."

Bob told me where to meet him, and I printed MapQuest directions for getting there. A coworker at FLW, Jason Sealock, was going with me, to photograph the fishing. Sealock had previously worked as a programmer for a major banking company in Arkansas. Talking with him, you could tell that he was a genius or close to one, even if he had left a six-figure tech job to work for a fishing magazine that paid about a third of the money. But Sealock said he couldn't stand that corporate world for one second longer, and he loved fishing besides. So, he quit at the bank and moved to Kentucky, and that put us in the company truck together, headed south to Mississippi to noodle for catfish with strangers that I'd been told were "rough around the edges."

I called Bob as we got closer, and he and his buddy Rick met us in the searing parking lot of a boat ramp, with the muddy Yazoo River flowing behind them. Bob was around 6 feet tall, with the build of a middle-aged man who worked outside, broad shoulders and a slight gut, and skin leathered by the sun. He had big hands—chain-sawing hands, as he was a tree trimmer—that were well suited for wrestling catfish. His narrow eyes and slight smirk betrayed a bit of Southern meanness, too, something I'd been around before. I knew within seconds that Bob would take me handfishing, but not as any sort of favor or to be featured in a magazine. He simply seemed amused by the idea of terrifying a skinny, 21-year-old magazine writer.

"Wade Junior. Damn, I don't know if he's big enough to hold onto a fish or not, do you?" he asked, speaking at Rick. "Water's still cold, so if we find one, it's probably going to be a blue."

That mention of "a blue" caused Rick to speak up. He was of about the same height as Bob but frail, with the slow movement of a man battling a deep illness. Rick had been a handfisherman himself for years, but he'd gotten sick—ALS, I believe—and it made him too weak to wrestle catfish. Still, he referred to himself as a "specialist" at riding in the boat, watching, and drinking beer. And all of that time on the water as an observer helped him act as an unofficial publicist for Bob and the catfish both. Ninety-eight pounds was the biggest flathead they'd ever caught, Rick said, but a blue cat half that size was a scarier critter.

Rick proudly showed off his own forearm, which was laced with scars. "That's all from catfish, mostly from flatheads," he said. "But those blue cats will cut you deep. We took this one old boy for the first time, and he reached in, and a big blue just hammered him. He came up, hand bleeding, and wouldn't go back down. We rode his ass pretty hard, though, and after about 10 minutes he finally went back. Thing about a big blue, once you piss it off, you can't hardly stop it from biting you. That fish came out and hit the guy right in the armpit before he ever even reached into the box. Almost cut his titty off. That guy wouldn't go back down at all after that. Needed a couple stitches, really."

But Bob didn't seem to suffer such calamities, according to Rick. "He's the only man I've ever seen who could grab a catfish barehanded and not even get scratched," Rick said. "He's so good because he can hold his breath so long. Shoot, sometimes Bob will be under for two minutes, and we'll think he's drowned, and then he comes up with two catfish at once, 80 pounds of fish on one arm, his hand run through the gills of one of them and holding the jaw of the other. That's no lie."

"I don't think I can hold my breath for two minutes," I said.

"You can't hold it two seconds if you're scared," Bob shot back.

"What about gloves?" I asked. "I brought some leather ones to wear. I just got married here a few weeks ago and need to be careful not to lose my new ring."

Bob glared as though he just might split my skull with his gaze alone. "No, you ain't wearing gloves," he said. "I might wear one, but if you're going to fish with us, you're going to do it the right way. If you catch one, your hands will be so sore and cut you won't be able to reach in your pocket for a week to get change. Get your mind right, Junior. Let's go eat, then we'll do some assing around."

Jason and I split the tab on company cards after we all dined at a steak house, and then Bob motioned for us to get into the back seat of Rick's pickup. "Assing around," we realized, was driving Delta backgrounds while Bob navigated and Rick drank whiskey and Soggy Bottom Boys' "Man of Constant Sorrow" played on the radio. "This is our redneck theme song," Rick said, and then he pulled over and declared that he was going to have a little drink but needed to find a cup first. He stepped out, rummaged in his truck bed, and produced an herbicide measuring container.

"I don't know if that's safe to drink out of or not," he said, staring at the numbers on the side of the cup. Bob snatched it from his hand, sniffed it, and said that it was fine and that Rick was sick anyway besides. Rick shrugged, stepped out again for a handful of ice from his cooler, and then pulled a bottle of bourbon whiskey from under his seat. He dumped several good sloshes of it into the cup, took a deep sip, smacked his lips in satisfaction, placed it between his knees, and continued driving.

"Where'd you say you're from, Junior? Kentucky? Cameraman, too?" Bob asked, never looking back at us.

"Yeah, Kentucky," I said.

"I'm from Arkansas, originally," Jason added.

"How those Yankee women look up there? Y'alls wives fat?"

"No, they're pretty good-looking wives," Jason said.

"Huh," Bob said. Then he hit Rick in the shoulder and motioned for him to turn. "That's it up there," he said.

We turned onto a gravel drive and followed it to a small, wooden cabin on the edge of a cypress brake. The sun was sinking, and Bob looked at us and said, "We gonna get out here for a while, both of you." Rick poured some more whiskey, and then both of them stepped out and walked toward the cabin. They paused near the water's edge, and Jason and I followed them but slowly, wondering why, exactly, we were there.

Bob stared out through the cypress trees with his arms crossed before turning again to look at me. He seemed to tower overhead despite being only a couple inches taller and with that constant, slight smirk, as if he were about to say something but was trying to decide first just how vicious it should be.

"Well, Junior, the fish are out there!" he said and then suddenly lurched toward me, grabbed the back of my shirt and belt, and picked me up clear off the ground, feigning throwing me into the water. Then he set me back down, howling with laughter. I took a step back from him and laughed myself, but it was fake, the sound a bullied kid might make to garner sympathy from a tormentor. Jason wasn't smiling at all.

The hum of a distant 2-stroke outboard broke the moment, and soon a johnboat came coasting into view. "There he is," Bob said, and when a man in the boat beached it onshore, Bob took a step toward him and looked inside. A 10-pound flathead was thrashing in the bottom. Bob leaned in and spoke to the man for a while, and when the conversation, one I couldn't hear, seemed to end, he grabbed the flathead by its lower jaw and hoisted it with one arm. "Hell, that one ain't even big enough to clean," he said. He chunked the catfish into the water, it flipping in the air before splashing down. Then he looked at me again. "We better get Junior here back to town so he can get a good night's sleep."

To this day, I don't know why we went to that cabin or who the man in the johnboat was. Back at the hotel, Jason and I agreed that we were both uncomfortable, scared even, and we talked about packing up and going home that very night.

But instead, we met Bob and his friends the next morning to go handfishing in the Yazoo River.

We rallied at a small café shortly after sunrise. Bob had parked his pickup out front, and he had a pair of snarling rat terriers yapping in the bed. Bob walked to the door of the café and then turned to the dogs. "Y'all stay there and hush," he said, and both dogs silenced immediately and stood shoulder to shoulder, stock still.

Jason and I followed Bob inside, where he was greeted by a crowd of locals, many of whom were apparently going fishing with us. The server was a pretty brunette, and Bob pointed right at her and leaned toward me and said aloud, "That's how they're grown in Miss'ippi, Junior." Jason and I again paid the tab, maybe for everyone in the café since they all seemed to know Bob, and it still wasn't clear who was going fishing and who wasn't. The terriers broke into hysterics again as soon as we stepped back outside, and it was plain by the blue, still sky overhead that we had a blistering hot day ahead of us—perfect weather, Bob said, for grabbing catfish.

Back at the launch ramp, we stepped into a flotilla of four War Eagle johnboats and began motoring upstream, Jason in one boat with one crew to photograph and me riding with Rick, Bob, and the terriers. Over the sound of the 2-stroke, I yelled out to ask Bob how long he'd been fishing the Yazoo—and I pronounced it Yah-zoo, as it seemed to be spelled.

"Damn, Junior, you can't help but sound like a Yankee," he said. "It's yeah-zoo, not yah-zoo. Long time. We run up and then use the current to come back down. Couldn't do it any other way. We've had so many fish in the boat before that it about sank us, and you wouldn't be able to run against the river with all that weight."

Bob and his crew built wooden boxes, roughly the size of coffins with a single entrance on the end, that they sank in the river and anchored to the bank or to logs with heavy cable. Catfish are cavity nesters, spawning in hollow logs, cut-out banks, beaver lodges, or perhaps wooden boxes. Being that large, Bob's catfish boxes could hold some exceptional specimens. He said, in fact, that was the primary thing that helped him catch bigger catfish than everyone else. Most handfishermen just don't make their boxes big enough.

The water in the Yazoo, being the color of creamed coffee, kept the boxes hidden, and they were scattered every couple hundred yards. The cables held them in place and also aided as handlines for reaching the deepest of the boxes, which were 15 feet down. Most, though, were 4 to 6 feet deep. Bob said he'd seen plenty of grown men jump in, follow the cable down, and then come up with the report, "I can't find the hole."

"They just don't want to find it," he said. "Lots of people don't."

After an hour of running, we finally slowed to a stop, and Rick grabbed a shoreline limb to hold the boat in place. The current was swift enough to bubble alongside the hull. Bob hopped into the water, looked up at me with his smirk, and said, "Well, you up."

I jumped in as well and was immediately swept downstream, past the box. I kicked and paddled my way back and grabbed hold of the black cable, which was looped over and clamped to a log on the shore. "Follow that cable down and reach inside. Don't let go of him when he bites you," Bob said.

I didn't want to be pegged as Junior, who couldn't even find the box, but when I took a breath and went under, it was like being tossed through a violent storm. The view changed from solid brown to black, depending on whether I opened my eyes. I followed the cable, and my lungs burned for air just as my hand brushed the top of the box. I sprung away from it and sputtered at the surface, struggling to speak.

"I can't find it," I said. Bob roared.

"Don't start that shit! Either find it or get back in the boat."

I decided I'd rather drown than chance getting back in the boat with Bob without finding the hole to the box. I dove again, pulled myself down with the cable, and finally discovered the entrance, which was maybe 20 inches wide. Opening my eyes, I could just see the cavern, foreboding and black and perhaps concealing something monstrous inside, a blue cat capable of biting off a titty. I plunged my hand into it, being out of breath already, and swept my palm across, deep as I could go. I felt mud and smooth, treated lumber and winced as I waited for a giant catfish to lurch forward and attack my hand, but none did. I pushed off the mud bottom to the surface once more, aching for oxygen.

"I found it," I gasped. "There's no fish in it, though." Bob's smirk widened slightly, and he simply dropped below the water's surface.

"Dude, you better hope there's no fish in there," Jason said from his boat.

Bob appeared again, though, and the smirk was gone.

"Junior's right. No fish in there," he said. "Let's go to the next one."

"It's good for the first one or two to be empty," Rick said after I pulled myself back into the boat. He'd cracked open a Busch Light, and it was as if he felt the sudden need to provide some counsel. "It gets you a little comfortable with it, and then *bam*, he'll come out and hit you! You'll swear it's an alligator in that box, first time you get bit."

We checked the next box, and it was empty, too, and so was the one after that. I dove out of and climbed back into the boat, over and again, sweeping my palm through every box and then waiting while Bob double-checked them just in case. Empty spots pass quickly when you're handfishing, and before long we were halfway back to the ramp without having touched a single fish.

As we idled along, Bob suddenly pointed to a giant water snake lumbering up the mudbank. He cut the tiller of the motor hard and swung the boat in toward the bank, leaning over the gunwale as he went, like a warrior counting coup. He grabbed the snake right in the middle with his outstretched arm and flung it into the boat, right at my feet, in one motion. I knew the snake wasn't a water moccasin and am not scared of snakes besides, but water snakes are ill-tempered, and this one was plenty big enough to draw blood. But biting or scaring me wasn't the intent. Bob's dogs needed to be fed. The terriers descended on the snake in a frenzy of yapping and blood and gore and snarls, ripping apart chunks of keeled-scale flesh and swallowing them whole.

"Them dogs love a snake," Bob said. And then he looked at me with no smirk at all. "Don't worry, Junior. We got some boxes left. We'll find you a fish."

But after a few hours I was tired just from the swimming, and the river's shoreline was looking familiar. We were close to town, near the launch ramp again, and I knew we were running out of chances. The reality of going home from my first field assignment with nothing more than pictures of me swimming was sinking in. "Bob, we need a fish for pictures," I said. "I'm probably just going to mess it up if we find one. You better check the rest of the boxes yourself." He nodded.

We were within sight of the boat ramp and at the second-to-last box when Bob hopped into the water, which was about chest deep, and waded toward a dead snag where the black cable was tied off. He eased underneath the surface and this time came up with a genuine smile.

"Get in the water, Junior," he said. "There's a yella cat in this one, about 25 pounds." Jason clawed for his camera, and the other boats idled into a circle around us. I hopped over the side of our vessel and waded toward Bob. "Get your mind right now," he said. "This is you chance. Don't let go of him."

The flathead lashed at my hand when I went underwater and reached inside the box, and briefly, I hooked two fingers onto its lower jaw. But the fish retreated just as fast, and I let go, coming to the surface for a breath but swinging both of my feet into the entrance of the box to block the fish if it tried to escape.

"He bit me!" I yelled.

"Well don't tell me about it, grab him!" Bob yelled. The noise from the other boats was hitting a frenzy, Jason's camera snapping, stomping feet on aluminum hulls, beer tabs popping, and men screaming under the influence of alcohol and heat and the promise of violence inflicted on a skinny writer but also, perhaps, cheering me on, too.

Underwater, though, that noise was all just a hum overhead. I reached inside the box, and it was as if the catfish was simply waiting for me, with its mouth slightly agape. My bare hand landed on its gill rakers, and I grabbed them, squeezing as hard as I could. The fish chomped down around my forearm, sandpaper teeth peeling skin as it twisted and thrashed, but I worked my left hand in then, behind the gill plate, and then locked the fingers of both hands together, inside the fish's head. This was a fight between that catfish and me, underwater, with no hook or line between us, and I knew something would have to tear, part of the fish or part of my arm, before I let go. I pulled the flathead out of the box, held it tight to my chest, and broke the water's surface slowly, where Bob was looking me in the eyes with a maniacal grin, and I gave him one back that was just as crazy.

"Get that camera ready," I hissed to Sealock. "'Cause I've got the son of a bitch."

I pulled the flathead up and into view and waded toward the nearest War Eagle, where Rick was standing, whooping, holding a beer in one hand, and thrusting the other into the air with a skinny, scarred arm. I slung the catfish over my shoulder and into the boat, with a backdrop of Mississippians screaming as if they'd just fought and killed an entire invading army. An iced Busch Light seemed to appear in my hands instantly—courtesy of Rick—and I snapped it open with two bloodied hands. When I turned back toward Bob, he'd extended his hand to shake my own. It was a firm handshake but friendly as you'd shake a buddy's hand after you haven't seen him in a while. "Junior, you all right," he said.

The bedlam and adrenaline subsided a bit, and one of the boats broke free from the flotilla and putted just across the river toward the ramp. I climbed back into the boat with Rick and Bob and sipped my beer and eyed the writhing flathead at my feet, the finest fish I'd ever seen. Jason was reviewing the images on his camera in the next boat and looking up at me and smiling. By the time my beer was down to a few warm suds, the men in the other boats were shouting at us.

"Hot damn, they found a fish for the cameraman, too," Bob said. We motored toward them, and Jason handed me the camera before hopping into the water himself, smiling slightly but looking more determined than anything. The genius programmer turned fishing writer and photographer slogged toward the box, a shallow one, a crazed Mississippian sitting on top of it, breaking the current with his ass and holding a beer as blood oozed from his knuckles.

"Big old blue cat in this one, cameraman!" he said. "You sure you want to reach in there? Just look at my hand! Hell, it'll take a month to heal! Reach right in there under my nut sack, and you'll find him."

Jason took a breath and lowered himself below the water, disappearing under a few bubbles. A thump rang out, the concussive sound of a big catfish biting a man's arm clear up to the elbow. But Jason didn't bail or even come up for air. To this day, he's one of the few people I've ever seen who caught a catfish by hand on his very first reach into a hole. The blue, bigger even than my flathead, shredded the back of Jason's arm, but he held on, tossing the fish into the nearest boat, and the frenzy of foot stomping and beers snapping and whooping continued to the ramp and in our heads for the entire drive home until I got back at 1:00 a.m. to knock on my apartment door.

The next week, Michelle and I were in Walmart when my cell phone rang, and my hand had scabbed over just enough to reach into my pocket to get it. I was shocked to see that Bob was calling me.

"Junior. That yellow shit coming out of your hand yet?" he asked. I told him that it was indeed healing up, itching now more than hurting, but that it hurt like a son of a bitch earlier in the week and, by God, I was wearing a glove next time. He laughed. "Well, you and cameraman better get your asses back down here then. It's got hot, and the flatheads are up. We caught the hell out of them yesterday. One of those days we nearly sunk the boat with so much weight."

I told Bob that I wanted to come down, but work was busy. Jason was traveling, photographing a bass tournament, and we had a magazine printer deadline coming up. "I understand being busy," he said. "One more thing. Be sure you mention Rick in your story. He used to be a hell of a handfisherman. I'm afraid he ain't going to live much longer."

I promised Bob that I would.

The Mississippi handfishing season faded with the summer, and I worked on my story all the while, one draft of it after the next. But the finished product, a version of what you've read here, wasn't a fit for the sanitized pages of *FLW Outdoors*, which were devoted to covering the NASCAR-like sport of tournament fishing. So, I pitched it to *Field & Stream* and landed my first assignment there.

I called Bob some months later to tell him about the upcoming story and also to talk about the boxes that I'd been working on over the winter to sink in Kentucky Lake. Fact was, since I'd left

Mississippi, I couldn't get handfishing out of my head. But Bob didn't return my call, the first or the second one, and finally, when I called third time, his wife answered, sounding stunned that I'd asked for Bob at all and then breaking into sobs. "Bob died," she said. "The lift bed of his dump truck, it killed him."

Jason had written down Rick's number, somewhere on a notepad in a camera case while we were fishing, and so I called him next. "There was more to the story than Bob getting killed," Rick said. "They about had him for murder. Found him dead under the lift bed of that truck, suffocated, after they'd questioned him. He was by himself when the accident happened. There was nothing wrong with the truck."

Archived news reports from the area said that police had found evidence of a land dispute between Bob and a local attorney. And in January, the attorney was in his own home when somebody shot him through the window with a shotgun, killing him dead. Police had questioned Bob, and then in February, Bob was found dead. Foul play wasn't suspected in Bob's accident, the stories said.

"I suppose that's how you'd expect a man like Bob to go out," Wade Bourne said to me later when we were talking about it. "Of all the stories I've done, those on handfishing are the ones I'm asked about the most. People are just mesmerized by it."

I grabbed my first catfish on Kentucky Lake the next summer, a flathead that was only a little smaller than the one I'd caught with Bob and Rick and Jason and the Mississippians down on the Yeah-Zoo River. I didn't wear a glove, and for a week after, my hands were so cut up and sore that it hurt to reach in my pocket to get change. All these years later, if you look carefully, you'll see that my arms are laced with scars. All from catfish.

THE VOODOO BOX

Some of the finest turkey hunting I've ever seen was in a reclaimed strip mine in Kentucky where the creeks ran orange from acid drainage but the spoil banks were thick with mayapples and morels come spring and crawling with wild turkeys, too. The mining roads made it easy to slip around quietly until you struck a bird.

Still, it wasn't easy hunting. Often you found yourself calling across the cuts, from the rim of one "high wall" to gobblers on the rim of another. An eastern wild turkey is notorious for its refusal to step over a small ditch or around a log in the trail when responding to a call. It would seem virtually impossible, then, to lure one across a massive, excavated canyon. But one morning I did just that, thanks to the sounds of a Lynch Fool Proof Model 101 box call. I was 15 and had gotten the call as a Christmas gift a few years before. It was a mahogany wood box with a unique, single-sided design. Each time I'd pull it from my vest, I'd read the inscription on the side, which said,

> *It's fool proof. It's set up for the yelp, cluck, put, whine, and cackle. It's semi-automatic. Read simple instructions. Patents pending. This box made and tested by M.L. Lynch Co., World's Champion Turkey Caller and Manufacturer, P.O. Box 377, Liberty, Mississippi.*

The design of my call from years ago was apparently no different than the original that M.L. Lynch sold back in 1940 and also no different than the Fool Proofs that you can still buy today at Walmart for about $50. As you'd expect from any call produced in large quantities, some Fool Proofs sound a little better than others. The call I had was positively magic. My buddy Matt Seymore called it my "Voodoo Box."

The birds in the strip mine that day—there were two of them—had sounded off at about 9:00 a.m., and sure enough, they were on the other side of a wide cut. Dad and I had been slipping up a mining road on our side when they gobbled, and he said, "No damn way those turkeys are coming off that high wall." But we sat down to try them anyway, Dad up ahead with his A5 pointed at the mining road and me 15 yards behind him with the Fool Proof.

I yelped, and the turkeys immediately gobbled and strutted into sight on the edge of the opposite high wall, swollen and shiny as a pair of ripe plums. I yelped again, and they gobbled and strutted along the edge, hung up as you'd expect. But then one of the turkeys cocked its head sideways and looked down, as if wondering how bad it would hurt to fall. Turkeys are surprisingly graceful in flight, and these could've easily set their wings and glided across the cut, but I suppose their judgment was clouded by thoughts of sex and violence. Dad and I watched in amazement as they leaned back on their feathered asses and slid off the high wall, like flatland tourists who have abandoned all shame at the end of a hike and have decided to slide down a mountain rather than walk.

The turkeys were soon out of sight, in the cut below us. I yelped again, and they roared back from the bottom, like demons emerging from hell, and then they charged straight up our side and into the mining road. Dad killed the biggest one at 20 steps, and he had to stand up and shout to stop the other one from violating its dead companion.

Such was the power of the Fool Proof's song that I carried it for 15 straight seasons after—and in multiple states. I eventually sat on it one morning in Kansas or Nebraska—I don't remember which—and broke it. I've had other box calls that were more expensive and to my ear sounded better but none that have called another gobbler off a high wall.

Bluewing Weather

A perfect storm for September teal needn't be much of a storm at all. This one simply brought an inch of needed rain and a taste of fall when it dropped daytime highs from near 90 degrees into the 70s.

I went scouting the next day, a week before the teal opener, and I saw the first flock before I even stopped the truck. They're mostly brown that time of year, save for the chalk-blue speculums that always betray them in flight. The flock lit with what must've been a thousand more ducks standing on the mudflat. It was a veritable bluewing buffet. As a river-fed reservoir recedes after a long, dry summer, mud shorelines are exposed, and they're teeming with vegetation, seeds, and invertebrates. The mud is sticky and pungent, a rich blend of decaying milfoil, fish, and, if you're lucky, duck droppings.

Bluewings are apt to leave at the slightest weather change, so I checked on them three more times before opening morning, like a new parent watching a baby sleep. They were there each time, and I also noticed a big, grassy island in the middle of their favored flat—the perfect place to hide.

The only problem I could foresee was the popularity of that hunting spot. I knew we'd have some competition.

By 2:30 a.m., I had the boat ready, and my buddies Tim and Ryan and I were leaving town, determined to be the first to the field. We've been called crazy for getting started at that hour. But to us, "crazy" is losing the best spot because you wanted an extra hour of sleep.

It was a short boat ride to the grass island, and we had minimal gear to carry. In the tall island grass, a folding stool and camo shirt provided plenty of concealment. I wore hip boots, but there've been hunts when shorts and Crocs were sufficient. There wasn't much to the decoy spread, either. I used a dozen Texas-rigged teal decoys, but you can use mallard hens and get the same effect. I stood in one spot and chucked the decoys out into two groups, with a 10-yard-wide landing space between them, 15 steps from our hide in the island grass. Tim grunted a nod of approval and staked a Mojo Dove in the landing zone. Given the choice between the wing spinner and standard blocks for teal hunting, I'd take the spinner. While I now have a Mojo Teal that looks better in photos than the odd-bird-out dove, I can't tell that it makes any difference to the live ducks. They love that dove.

We drank coffee in the dark for 30 minutes before the next truck pulled up to the boat launch. A 2-stroke outboard gurgled to a start, and soon the boat was bobbing toward us. We shined a flashlight from our hide and listened to muffled cussing as the boat redirected its course to another spot.

Two more sets of headlights pulled to a stop at the ramp, and soon another vessel—this one propelled by a mud motor—was on the way. We shined our light, but they kept coming, finally gliding to a stop outside our decoys.

"We've already got this spot, guys," I yelled at them.

I heard a reply in the dark: "Dammit, is that you, Brantley?"

It was two more of our buddies, Danny and Dan. We told them that we'd whip their asses if they came up there, but at the same time we were clearing out room for them to sit with us on the grass island.

"I've been watching these ducks for a week," Dan said as they settled in. "There's been a bunch of them. I'm glad we don't have to fistfight a bunch of rednecks for this spot."

Half a dozen more boats motored by us, and then, during the 30 minutes before shooting light, all went quiet.

A bluewing hen quack is unmistakable—it has a fast rhythm and is at once high-pitched and raspy, like a sarcastic laugh. Ducks were splashing amid our decoys as the sky lightened, and several hens were quacking together. The birds in the spread flushed before the legal minute, but that gave us just a bit of extra light before the next flock—at least a dozen birds—roared in from behind us, a few feet over our heads. We hit them with teal quacks of our own. They banked sharply out front before swarming around the motorized dove. Tim fired the first shot and dropped two. The flock knotted together and sprang skyward. We all come up shooting and killed seven total. Tim nailed two more—his limit of four in three shots.

"I guess I'm done," he said, casing his shotgun. There was no time to feel sorry for him because the next flock was bearing down fast. Within 20 minutes, we were all casing our guns and gathering spent hulls. Teal were still buzzing past our heads as we picked up the dead ducks and decoys and took pictures.

The air became a little unsettled later that morning, and by the afternoon, a stiff breeze was blowing. Another cold front was brewing. I pulled up to the ramp just before sunset with binoculars, thinking of hunting the mudflat again the next morning. There were plenty of feathers washed against the grass island. But not a teal in sight.

The Lion Hunters

Miles Fedinec eyed me with a contempt that's normally reserved for little league umpires. I was at the SHOT Show, working for Realtree Camouflage, and had been ushered into a small meeting room where Miles was impressing my boss with pictures of a mountain lion that had been treed by Walker hounds.

"I think this guy could be a true expert source on Western hunting in some of your articles," my boss said to me, showing Miles off as if he were a trophy fish. But he was a Colorado hunting guide and in his late twenties, my age, and we seemed to detest one another immediately. When the meeting adjourned and it was just Miles and I standing there, he looked me square in the eyes and said that he'd guided a bunch of outdoor writers, and every one of them was full of shit. It crossed my mind to take a swing at him right there, but that would've been a real mess. Miles is a short guy—I've got 4 inches on him at least—but he always seems to be running on new plugs and fresh fuel. We eyed each other for a minute before separating, and I thought, "Damned if I'm ever calling that little asshole for anything."

But then, Michelle said she wanted to hunt a mountain lion, more than anything else. Miles was the closest thing I knew to a lion guide, and so I called him and said that if he'd take us hunting, I'd write a magazine story about him, and he'd probably stay booked up for years to come.

"I already told you outdoor writers were full of shit," he said. "But I guess you can come out, and we'll try to tree a cat."

Among hunters, there are dog people—those who love to watch a pointer get birdy or a Lab make a long retrieve—over just about anything else in the field. Among the dog people, there are houndsmen, who don't always get to see their dogs working but love listening to them. The hounds could be tiny beagles chasing cottontails, or blue ticks treeing coons, or Catahoulas baying up pigs. Larry, Michelle's dad, had redbone coonhounds, a male named Red and a female named Little Red, and sometimes he'd be gone into the wee hours of the morning, hunting with them. I was never taken with a particular love of hunting dogs, but Michelle was—and of hounds in particular.

But as much as that, Michelle wanted to see a big cat. Mountain lions are one of the most elusive animals in North America, but they're far more common throughout the West than many realize. Plenty of locals go their entire lives without ever seeing one in the wild. Miles said that in all of his life and in all of the hunting he'd done, he'd seen only one lion cross the road, ever. Mostly, if you want to see a live cat and certainly if you want to have a chance at tagging one, you hunt them with hounds.

Lion hunting is tightly regulated in most states where it's allowed, and lion meat is pretty good, similar to pork if you can get past the hint of litter box. In Colorado, harvesting all of the meat from a lion is a legal requirement, too. Before our hunt, Michelle had to take a mountain lion identification course to prove she should could distinguish cubs from adults and females with cubs from barren animals. We also had to be aware of the harvest quotas in various units. Once a quota is met in a given area, the unit is closed for the remainder of the season. Lion hunters therefore have to call and check in for whatever units they're planning to hunt each day, just to be sure they're still open.

Months ahead of the hunt, Michelle began a daily workout regimen of running and weight lifting since we'd be hunting in elevations above 6,000 feet and often in hostile terrain. We booked a flight to Colorado on Christmas Day.

Miles's bachelor pad was just what you'd expect, a modest house on a 40-acre spread in the high desert outside Craig, with walls adorned with taxidermy, including a tanned zebra skin and a woodstove. Among the first things he told us was that the shitter didn't flush right and to be careful not to clog it. The plan would be to strike out at daylight each morning, covering mountain trails by truck and snowmobile in an effort to cut a fresh lion track. Miles didn't have dogs of his own—and didn't much care for lion hunting—but he had several lion-hunting buddies who did have dogs and who were out searching for tracks at the same time we were.

Even among houndsmen, lion hunters are a peculiar breed. They live for running their dogs, yes, but lion tags are generally limited to one per hunter, per season, and you're not allowed to chase the cats without a tag. Because of that, many lion hunters are hesitant to actually shoot a lion themselves, and so knowing a hunter who's in possession of a tag that they want to fill is a hot commodity. Still, it couldn't be said that the lion hunters were working together that week in any sort of way. On the contrary, they all seemed to hate one another and simply wanted a chance to cut the first track and prove that their hounds were better than all the rest.

"Most of these guys are assholes in their own right, and they'd probably fight each other if they crossed paths out there,"

Miles said as we drove a mountain road, looking for tracks. "But without fresh snow, it might take a week to cut a track, so we're casting a wide net."

The mornings were frigid, as you'd expect in the Rockies in December, with single digits turning the existing snow into a dense crust. Once or twice, we cut old tracks and summoned buddies with dogs, but the trails went cold quickly. Michelle and I rode along with Miles in his truck, drank coffee, and told stories, and after a couple days I decided that I didn't want to punch him in the mouth anymore.

We were set to run a snowmobile through a mountain trail on the third morning, but as we approached the trailhead, another truck, with a trailer and dog box, was already parked.

"That's Russ Berhman and his kid, Talin," Miles said. "He's a damn good lion hunter."

Russ was maybe 50 years old, with shaggy salt-and-pepper hair and dressed in wool bibs. Talin had a similar haircut but bright blond, as he was 16. Miles slowed his pickup to a stop, and introductions were made. "We've already been all through that trail," Russ said. "No good tracks to speak of. It's going to be hard to find one if we don't get some snow."

We only had another two days to hunt before we were due to fly back home. Russ mentioned that a buddy of his had been hunting for cow elk the day before in a different unit and had actually seen a cat slipping across a canyon at daybreak. He said that he might spend some time there the next morning to see if he could cut the track and that if he found something, he'd call.

"I didn't know lion hunting would be so boring," Michelle said as we settled into bed that night. "We haven't done anything except ride around in the truck for three days."

The next morning, we awoke with renewed hope, as an inch of fresh snow had fallen just before daybreak. Miles called to check the day's lion quota, and decided that we'd try to cut tracks on some public land north of Craig. We worked our way up the mountainside slowly, stopping on occasion to double-check scuffs and drags in the snow for hints of a lion. Nothing. As the sun rose and disappointment began setting in again, Miles suddenly got a call. "We've got to go," he said, hanging up. "Russ Behrman just cut a smoking fresh track."

Miles called his lion-hunting buddy, Casey, who'd been out all week looking for tracks as well, and told him we were headed out to find Russ and to follow us in case we needed more dogs. We bounced down the mountain trails and onto the blacktop, where Miles floored it. Russ was an hour away and holding his dogs back until we got closer, as regulations prohibit treeing a lion and keeping it there until the hunter is present.

The terrain changed from alpine to high desert, and we saw Russ's truck parked on a dirt road up ahead. I expected to see bouncing hounds on leashes, but instead Russ and Talin were standing next to their flatbed, looking through a spotting scope mounted to a tripod.

"I don't know what the hell is going on here," Miles said, but we pulled to a stop and stepped out.

"You won't believe this," Russ said. "We cut the track and then saw that cat go across the valley there and up into that cave. Look through that spotter."

I leaned over to look through the lens, which was pointed at a tiny cave in the face of a cliff, 200 feet above flat ground. A large rock lay across the entrance of the cave, and there on that rock, sitting in the sun, was a mountain lion. Michelle looked through the spotter and grinned with excitement, but I had to wonder, *How in the hell are we going to get up there to that cat?*

"I think we just climb up there and try to sneak in close for a shot," Miles said. "And then if that doesn't work out, we turn the dogs loose."

Russ agreed. "You know the cat's in that cave. No telling how far it'll go if we turn the dogs out now. We'll glass from down here while you guys sneak up there."

Michelle had planned to shoot a cat, if we treed one, with her Hoyt compound bow. But this was no place for a bowhunt. Miles grabbed his scoped AR-15 from the truck and racked a .223 cartridge into the chamber. I checked the loads in my .44 Magnum Ruger Blackhawk and grabbed my pack and camera, and Miles, Michelle, Talin, and I made our way toward the base of the cliff.

We made most of the climb up a cut, which was steep but not of a lethal grade. Michelle and I labored behind, flatlanders struggling to keep up and catch our breath in the high altitude. Miles and Talin waited for us to catch up, and we rallied just 30 yards below the cave.

"That's our only way up there," Miles whispered, pointing at the cliff face. Across it, there was a slight ledge, just wide enough for a boot, and enough dimples in the rocks above to serve as handholds. As if it had been placed there, a juniper tree protruded from just below the cave, and above it, we could see the bottom of the flat, sunny rock, where we believed the cat was still sitting, sunning itself.

Talin turned and glassed through his binoculars back down at Russ in the valley below, who was staring back at us through the spotting scope. Talin nodded and whispered, "Dad says the cat is still sitting right up there."

Michelle looked at the cliff and didn't say anything. It was a sheer drop to the ground below, not survivable. "We can't do this," I said. "It's not worth it."

Miles shrugged. "It's a bad spot. But this is your chance at a lion. Up to you."

Michelle looked at me, and then at Miles, and then up toward the cliff. "Let's go," she said.

Talin went first, scooting along the ledge with his belly pressed against the cliff, feeling slowly for handholds above. He passed the juniper and waved for us to follow. Miles went next, holding the AR with his right hand and bracing himself with the left. Michelle went next, and I scooted along last in line.

Miles reached for the juniper, grabbed the trunk, and pulled himself up, balancing with the rifle the whole way. The tree uprooted just as he scrambled over the top of it, dirt trickling over our shoulders and rendering it useless as a handhold. Miles lay prone at the edge of the cave entrance, concealed by the sunning rock, and no more than 15 steps from the cat, which we still couldn't see but assumed was still there. He motioned for Michelle's hand, but she was too short to reach.

"Stretch as much as you can," I whispered to her and motioned for Talin's help. We each pressed against a butt cheek and pushed, lifting Michelle toward Miles, her boots kicking bits of rock that bounced onto our hat brims and then tumbled off the face, falling so far we couldn't hear them hit below. Miles grabbed Michelle around the wrist and pulled as we pushed, and then she was laying prone on the rock next to him. I saw them rise slowly to their knees, and Miles handed her the rifle and pointed up above.

"Listen," he whispered to her. "One way or another that cat is coming out of that cave, and he's either going to come right at us or go over the top. You've got to keep your cool. Don't panic and knock me off here. If we fall, we're both dead."

Michelle took the AR from Miles and checked that the scope magnification was on the lowest power. She then flipped the safety lever down to Fire, shouldered it, and slowly rose to her feet with the gun at low ready. The mountain lion was staring at them, 10 steps away.

"Kill it!" Miles hissed, and she had the crosshairs on the base of the cat's neck, just under the chin. She pulled the trigger. I heard the rifle *click* from the cliff below, where I held on and watched in helplessness as the cat poised itself.

"It misfired!" Michelle gasped, but without giving up a step. The cat stared at them and tensed as Miles grabbed the rifle, ripped the bolt back, and let it fly, slamming it home on a fresh round and dropping it back into Michelle's hands. As she shouldered the gun again, I saw the cat leap up and onto the sunning rock and then turn and scale the vertical cliff behind in one seemingly fluid motion. Michelle fired as it did, and I saw blood fly from the cat just before it disappeared over the peak of the cliff.

"She hit him in the ass!" Talin yelled. Michelle and Miles sprang up and ran ahead, out of sight. I turned and began scaling back across the face to the cut where we'd climbed up. I heard hounds down below and knew they were being turned out to track the lion. "We gotta go!" Talin yelled, breezing past me and down the mountain. I looked back up the hill for Michelle and Miles but couldn't see them. So, I ran. I neared Russ's truck at the bottom, heaving for air. Talin was already in the front seat, seeming barely winded. "Get in, dude, they're hot after him!" Russ laughed as I clawed for the door handle and got inside.

"Gun didn't go off," I gasped. "I don't know where they all got to."

"She hit him in the tail before he went over the cliff," Russ said. "Don't worry, Casey's dogs will have him up a tree here in just a bit. Miles and your wife are chasing them now. We'll drive around and meet up with them." I slugged a bottle of water and rode in the back seat, out of breath, disoriented, and still unclear on exactly what all was happening.

Casey had driven around the hillside and turned out his hounds, which picked up the cat's track immediately. It had crossed a mile of open, snowy meadow by the time Miles and Michelle came down the back of the hillside, and they jumped in with Casey and drove close as they could but then had to stop near a fence and run again. The hounds were baying frantically in a juniper thicket up ahead, and Casey yelled that they sounded treed. The snow was up to Michelle's knees, but she pressed on, stumbling, running, and doing her best to reach the melee in the junipers.

The hounds were swarming under a thick tree, with one of them having climbed low limbs to 10 feet high in the canopy. It bayed at something above, and then a limb broke, and it fell in a shower of snow, righting itself immediately and falling back into the fray, with its hind leg streaking red in the snow, as it had torn a dewclaw in the fall. Above the dogs, the limbs shook slightly; even in that moment the cat managed to remain concealed.

Michelle was catching her breath, but she shouldered her rifle and searched for an opening. "Miles, I don't have a clear shot," she said. Hounds bawled at a frenzy.

"Put it on fur and shoot before he jumps tree," Miles said. She could see the tiniest hint of brown through the greenery and she fired. The cat faltered and sprang into the open, across a limb, and the AR popped twice more. The lion sagged and fell, hit through the lungs with both of the final bullets.

The dogs were still in hysterics when Russ, Talin, and I finally reached the tree, but by then Michelle, Miles, and Casey were relaxed, reliving the moment and taking pictures of an animal that few people are ever lucky enough to see, even though they're out there, hiding in the shadows and the caves. The ultimate reward for a houndsman. Or a houndswoman. The Lion Hunters would move on the next day, hoping for fresh snow, looking for a new track and for someone else with a tag that they wanted to fill. I looked at Miles and smiled and thanked him. He smiled back and said you're welcome, and we shook hands.

On the way home, he mentioned that he'd never hunted whitetails in Kentucky or turkeys anywhere at all.

The Bluegill Date

Michelle and I were 17 the first time we ever went bluegill fishing together. The best bream spot I knew of back then was the Flat Pond, a 2-acre gem hidden in the timber a couple of miles from home and about a half mile from the Bass Hole. Just getting there was an adventure that required a half-hour trek through woolly, reclaimed mine country, but I didn't mind the walk or even baiting all the hooks for the chance to fish with her.

Turns out, Michelle could bait her own hook just fine. Larry had taught her how. We caught a bunch of bluegills, and a bonus 3½-pound largemouth that was the biggest bass Michelle had ever seen. The date was going great—until she looked down at her tennis shoes and saw that they were crawling with a hundred or more Lone Star ticks, among the laces and creeping slowly down into the soles. She screamed and kicked the shoes off, and I dunked them into the pond, but that didn't faze the ticks in the slightest. "I'd rather walk home barefoot!" she said.

I followed her, carrying the poles, tackle, and stringer—bass included since Michelle wouldn't hear of turning it loose. We walked on, and for a while we didn't say much. When we finally reached the truck, Michelle stopped to rub her bloodied feet. I expected her to list the many reasons why this would be our first and last fishing date. Instead, she looked at me and said, "That really is a big old bass."

A girl like that doesn't come around every day.

Six years later, newly married and broke, Michelle and I lived in a one-bedroom apartment near Kentucky Lake. We fished almost every day, usually for bluegills. It wasn't long before a job change carried us to Memphis. The bream fishing in the Tennessee oxbows was even better than the barbecue and blues, but it wasn't home. We moved back to Kentucky less than two years after we left—but it wasn't to settle down. Michelle wore a bracelet that said Free Spirit, and we lived by that—traveling all over the country, hunting ducks in Louisiana, mountain lions in Colorado, gators and hogs in Florida, and whitetails, turkeys, and flatheads around home. And we still fished for bluegills every spring, same as we'd done since we were 17. Our folks finally quit asking if we were going to have kids.

One fall afternoon in 2013, I walked into the living room and found Michelle lacing up her hunting boots. A good cold snap had set in, and she wanted to do some rattling in her stand.

"Also," she added, "I'm pregnant." A writer prides himself on always having something to say. Right then, I had nothing.

Our child was due June 18. Toward the end of May, Michelle reminded me that it was the first spring since we were 17 that we hadn't gone bluegill fishing. It didn't matter that she was now weeks beyond the point of doctor-recommended johnboat rides; Michelle wanted to catch some bluegills, and she was going fishing, with or without me.

I've never negotiated waves more carefully than I did that day. Michelle and I struggled with the fishing at first. One bed produced a dozen keepers, but the others were empty—at least, we didn't catch anything. Distracted, I reeled in more than a few clean hooks. I kept asking Michelle, "Are you okay?"

"If I go into labor, I'll tell you," she eventually said. "Stop asking."

We fished on, and for a while we didn't say much. Michelle braced her swollen ankles on the gunwale and used her belly as a table to bait her hooks. She kept fishing, and on the first of what would be many "last casts," she found the best bluegill bed of the day. Soon she was catching a fish every minute and smiling like she was 17 again back at the flat pond. As the sun began to set, our wire basket—now genuinely heavy—buzzed with bream. Usually at the end of the day, Michelle quits first. That time, though, we just kept going till it was too dark to see our corks.

William Anse Brantley arrived a day late, on June 19. People said he had my eyes and Michelle's nose. We've always had stories to tell him, including why there's a 3½-pound bass mounted on the wall.

Chapter Four
On Assignment

King of the Swamp

My Argentine guide, Cally, pulled me aside and revealed three shotgun shells in his left hand, as if they were contraband. The crimps on all of the shells were bulged slightly, betraying some tabletop handloading work that Cally had been doing on them, likely with a flat screwdriver as the primary tool. He opened his right hand to reveal the "why" behind the bulged crimps: half a dozen steel ball bearings.

We were going to hunt capybara that evening in a little feeder creek of the Rio Salado behind the camp. But the No. 7½ lead shot we'd been using for ducks and doves probably wouldn't be enough to knock over a 100-pound rodent. Since we didn't have a rifle in camp or any real buckshot, Cally improvised, pouring the bird shot out of the three shells, replacing it with as many ball bearings as he could stuff inside the hulls, and then pressing the crimps back shut. Honestly, we might've been better armed with the bird shot. And I wondered if firing such a load through the expensive Benelli shotgun I'd been using would void the warranty on it. Still, I took the shells from Cally with a knowing nod, stuck them in my pocket, and continued treating them as contraband.

I was there as a guest of Benelli on assignment to write a story about wing-shooting with their new Super Black Eagle III shotgun in the legendary dove fields and duck marshes of Argentina, where hunting ducks with lead shot is still perfectly legal, and so too is hunting capybaras, even though not many Americans travel all that way to do it.

But Cally and I had become fast friends the first morning out, and I learned that killing a capybara was high on his list of priorities, even higher than killing a bunch of ducks. The giant rodents are a delicacy among local hunters and rural folks in Argentina, same as nutria rats. There were even jars of pressure-canned capybara meat for sale in some roadside service stations.

Skinning Catfish in Mary's Kitchen

We'd had a great duck hunt that morning, with swarms of South American waterfowl finishing over our decoys, Brazilian teal being the stars of the show. As we were walking out, mud sucking at our waders, Cally said something lengthy to me, but in Castilian Spanish, which I couldn't understand. "No comprende, buddy," I said, and he repeated it and made a motion of shouldering a gun. I shrugged—still didn't know—and he smiled and held up a hand, gesturing as if to say, "Just hang on a minute, Gringo," and we kept walking. Marta, the camp host and translator, was waiting for us at the truck, and I asked her to tell me what it was that Cally was trying to say. She spoke to him, and he repeated what he'd said to me.

"Oh, Cally just wants to know if you'd like to go hunt capybara with him tonight in the ditch, back behind the camp," she said. I thought maybe I'd seen a capybara in a zoo before, and I knew they were swampland creatures, similar to a beaver but three times the size and lacking the paddle tail.

"You tell Cally that I said, 'Hell yes, I want to hunt capybara,'" I said. Then I looked at Cally. "Capybara. Muy bueno. Amigo."

Marta said something else in Spanish, and Cally gave me a thumbs-up. Then she looked at me again. "I bet you get one. Cally's the best guide we have," she said. "The younger guys call him 'King of the Swamp.'"

Cally was maybe 50 years old, lean and in shape, and confident enough to usher an American client away from the supper table early to walk back toward the ditch behind camp. He lugged a small outboard motor, maybe a 2.5 horsepower, under one arm and had a 2-liter soda bottle filled with blue, mixed 2-stroke gas under the other. It was July, late winter in Argentina, and chilly enough to warrant the hand-knitted stocking cap he wore almost all of the time.

We parted reeds on the bank to reveal a worn fiberglass skiff with wooden 2 by 6 boards as bench seats and a cut-off yellow jug in the bottom for bailing water. Cally tightened the little motor to the transom and began cranking at the recoil starter. The motor wouldn't fire. He finessed the choke, squinted his eyes, cranked some more, and muttered what I assumed were profanities in Spanish.

"Damn, Cally, if only we had road signs here to shoot, I'd swear we were back home in Kentucky," I said.

He looked at me and said, "Will. No comprende." The "I" in "Will" was emphasized, so that it sounded more like "Weel" than "Will." I laughed, motioned like I was pull-starting a motor, and he turned back to the little outboard, which finally sputtered to life in a great plume of white smoke and a rainbow-colored oil slick. Cally removed his knitted hat to wipe sweat from his brow, then gave me a thumbs-up and motioned for me to sit in the bow of the boat.

We pushed away and began motoring down the ditch, which was maybe 10 feet wide, having obviously been channelized, and lined on both banks with reeds. I fished the crimped ball-bearing buckshots from my pocket, showed them to Cally so that he knew I was indeed using them, and thumbed them into the Benelli, secretly thankful that it was a media demo gun on loan and not something I'd paid good money for myself.

"Cally, where should I try to shoot a capybara?" I asked. His eyes narrowed, and I knew he didn't understand what I was saying but was struggling to try and figure it out.

I held up the gun and said, "Capybara. Bang! Muerto! Head or heart?," and I pointed to the side of my own head and then to my own chest. Cally nodded knowingly then and pointed to his own head.

We motored up the ditch for an hour, and Cally scooped water out of the boat with the yellow jug several times and unscrewed the top on the 2-liter bottle to pour mixed gas into the outboard's internal tank. But it was a dull trip, with the occasional caiman on the bank and some shorebirds but no giant rodents. The sun was beginning to sink, and though I had a flashlight, we were miles from camp with a motor that was sketchy and in remote South

America at that. As the light faded, Cally suddenly hit the kill switch on the motor, and we drifted along, slowly.

"*Weel!*" he whispered and pointed ahead. The shoreline reeds thrashed and shook, and some unseen critter huffed and fled into the thicket.

"Capybara?" I whispered, and Cally nodded. He again cranked the little motor, which was firing good now, and we putted ahead, with scarcely enough light to see. Directly, he again shut it off, and we coasted, and then I looked to my left, and there stood the most impressive rat I've ever seen, 100 pounds of fur and fat, standing on its hind legs, holding a tangle of green reeds and staring at me.

"*Weel!*" Cally hissed, but I'd already shouldered the Benelli and clicked the safety and leveled the orange bead just under the critter's chin in one fluid motion. The ball-bearing load went off with a *pop* in lieu of the expected 12-gauge boom, evidence that the hand crimping had affected the pressure of the shell and perhaps spilled some of the gunpowder, too. But we were close, only 5 yards or so from the capybara, and the steel ball bearings hit the beast and sent it tumbling into the water in a thrashing heap. Cally whooped and yelled something in Spanish, and I whooped and yelled something similar in Kentuckian, then racked the bolt on the shotgun and dropped the empty hull into the water at my feet, which really needed to be bailed again with the yellow jug. Even the Benelli, legendary for its reliability, wouldn't cycle those Argentina capybara loads.

But that didn't matter because we only needed the one of them to return to camp as conquistadors, with a capybara in tow. I stuck the other two in my pocket for later—I didn't know what Cally had planned for the next evening—and then helped him break a large limb from a deadfall on the bank. We used the limb as a fishing pole of sorts to guide the dead, floating rodent toward the boat. We both grabbed a leg and pulled the critter over the gunwale, where it splashed into the water at our feet, staining it red. The King of the

Swamp raised his hand for a high five and said something else in Spanish, and I said, "Hell yeah, let's take this thing back to camp and eat it!," and although neither of us knew exactly what the other was saying, two hunters from opposite sides of the globe knew exactly what it all meant.

Mule Deer Are Easy

I've got a shoulder mount of a fine 4×4 mule deer buck, and if I look at him from just the right angle, I'll swear that he's smirking. Shooting that buck was like backlashing on the first cast of the day but catching a 10-pound bass nonetheless or peaking in high school. It was the second time I ever hunted with Miles, my first time hunting mule deer, and, in fact, one of my first times going out West for big game. I'd never even seen a good mule deer buck before.

Miles had put up a ground blind on the edge of an alfalfa field where he'd been watching that deer feed every day for a month. A young guide trying to make a name for himself, he had invited me to Colorado to hunt on the condition that I write a story about it for *Field & Stream*. We still weren't positive that we even liked one another, but Miles had done his part. The buck ambled to within 25 yards, and I shot him through the heart with my bow. I then looked at Miles, declared that "mule deer hunting is easy," and tipped him $30.

I returned home from that hunt full of piss and vinegar. Michelle got pregnant immediately, and we brought our firstborn home right around the same time we welcomed my mule deer shoulder mount. One day, as I was scrubbing baby shit out of a couch cushion, Michelle looked at the mule deer mount and said, "I swear that thing is smirking at you."

I had to pay a lot of dues before killing another mule deer. I wrote so many stories about Miles that Colin Kearns, the editor in chief of *Field & Stream*, put a moratorium on even mentioning his name in the magazine. The ban was eventually lifted after Miles pulled Colin aside at the SHOT Show, got him good and liquored up, and then pointed to me and said, "Look, I'm about the only one who can stand to hunt with him. If you want him to tell stories, it has to be this way."

I'd gone back to Colorado almost every year to hunt antelope or elk, but several years passed before I hunted mule deer again. Miles called to tell me he had a line on a leftover archery deer tag. There were a lot of nice bucks running around, and he suspected I'd have a good time chasing them in early September, when they were still in bachelor groups. So, I bought the tag.

I missed two bucks, both longer shots than I should've taken, and screwed up half a dozen other stalks. It wasn't too tough to get within 75 yards of a bedded muley, and some people can kill them from there with a bow, but I can't. Much closer than that, and the critters would jump to their feet, as if triggered by an electric current to their short hairs. Then they'd stot away and stop at 150 yards to look back and smirk.

On the last morning of that hunt, I maneuvered around a group of four bucks, including one bruiser that was meandering toward a fence gap. I got between them and the gap and drew my bow as the big buck's antlers swayed into view. I was sitting on my knees in the brush, and the buck picked me out instantly, maybe a half second before I settled into my anchor point. He was just 25 yards away when he saw me. He broke into a full-on gallop and didn't stop for 200 yards. I went home without a buck.

The next fall, I cashed in some preference points on a muzzleloader tag and returned to hunt the same unit with an open-sighted rifle and plans on being picky. Problem was, there were only about a third of the deer in the area that I'd seen in the past. I finally got a chance at a nice 5×5 on the third evening and blew the shot at 130 yards. The following day, I crept to within 50 yards of two nice bedded bucks. I was proud of that stalk and figured venison was as good as in the cooler. As the deer stood up, I shouldered my gun and cocked the hammer.

Both bucks turned broadside, and the bigger of the two stared at me as the primer popped with a hiss, but the gun didn't fire—it was one of the few times in my life I've ever had a muzzleloader misfire in the field. Again, they stotted away, and though I couldn't see their smirk, I'm sure they were making one. On the last morning, I spotted another good buck a few ridges over and thought, "finally" as I snuck into position. I could see his forks poking above a rise 70 yards away and knew he was feeding right to an open flat not 50 yards from me. I waited with my gun at the ready.

But then the forks disappeared, and I didn't see the buck again. Thirty minutes later, I craned my neck up for a peek, only to see a bowhunter glassing back at me from exactly where the buck had been. The guy lowered his binoculars and then flipped me off, there in the distance, as if I was the one who'd messed up his hunt. Once again, I went home without a buck.

I did finally kill a good mule deer the next fall, when my friends at Browning took me on a hunt in Nebraska. There in the Sandhills, my guide and I kicked a giant buck up out of a thicket, and I plowed the deer over at about 25 yards with a 6.8 Western. "Man, talk about lucky, stumbling into that buck right there," my guide said. "I've never seen that deer before."

I sent Miles a picture and eventually called to tell him the story. I didn't describe it as a difficult hunt, but I thought of that shoulder mount back home, the smirking, and all the years and mess-ups in between. I didn't say one word about mule deer being easy.

Nora and the Moose

Devin McInnis wanted to drive his Jeep across the icy beaver pond. "It's 2 miles up that trail on the other side to the cutover where I think the moose are," he said. But it was 30 miles in the other direction to the nearest help—his mother's house. I envisioned bubbles as the Jeep's roof was engulfed in the brown-water abyss.

"I'm good with parking here and walking, buddy," I said.

We'd seen plenty of moose tracks there the day before, but the ones we'd cut in the last 45 minutes of light were sharply defined and punctuated by black spatter from the mud underneath the snow; McInnis and I knew the moose that made them wasn't far off. "The rut's over, but we still might get a bull to check out a call," he said. We followed the tracks a couple hundred yards into the timber, and I stood next to a tree with my rifle while McInnis made a long estrous-cow call: *Mmmwwaaaahhhh.*

I wanted to hear a branch break, to see something black and massive lumber out of the bush. But the North Woods were just silent, still, and cold. McInnis was undeterred. "We need to be here at daylight tomorrow," he said. "I bet he's in that cutover."

Northwest Alberta is bleak and beautiful—a place where wolves and bears and beavers live alongside tough Canucks like McInnis. The countryside is a mix of dark Canadian bush and rolling crop fields, and it's teeming with whitetails, mule deer, elk, and Canada moose—including some good bulls.

McInnis and I picked our way across the pond dam on foot. We reached the trail on the other side and immediately cut fresh tracks. "Cow and a calf," he whispered. He lit a cigarette and watched the smoke billow and roll back into our faces. "Wind's good."

Ten minutes later, the two moose that had made the prints erupted from the brush along the trail shoulder. They weren't visible for more than a few seconds before vanishing again into the bush, their black hides perfect camouflage in such a dark place. We continued along the trail, and the sign became more abundant—and not all of it was from cows. I noticed saplings big as my wrist broken off at chin height. McInnis said there was an intersection with another trail ahead, and he wanted to call before we got to it. We shuffled to a stop, and he scarcely had made a full cow call before we heard the crack of antler on a tree.

Without a word, we hustled forward for a clear view down the second trail. I caught a flash of antler moving through the trees to our right, and within seconds a bull moose trotted into plain view in the trail, 180 yards away. There was no time to kneel for a rest. I shouldered my rifle, a Winchester XPR in .300 Win Mag, dropped the crosshair onto the bull's chest, and fired offhand. The moose wheeled around, and I worked the bolt and fired a second shot over his back. Instead of disappearing into the trees, the bull just stopped. I bolted in the final shot, took a breath, settled the crosshair, and again hit the bull in the lungs. The moose turned once more and fell dead in the trail.

We walked up on the bull, and McInnis slapped me on the shoulder. "That's a pretty good bull, eh!" he said. Then he lit a cigarette and held it in his smile. When you're accustomed to whitetails, walking up on something the size of a moose is intimidating. You've seen the tracks and sign—but not until its full form is there in front of you can you grasp the size of this animal that seems ghostlike in the bush. You think to yourself, "Only in a place this wild."

The bull's rack measured 42 inches across, a good average for the area and outstanding to a guy who'd planned on shooting the first legal moose he saw. We took some pictures, and I quickly realized it wasn't an animal you can just move around for a better angle. As the adrenaline settled, we began discussing the beaver pond again. I assumed we'd be hauling quarters out on our backs. But McInnis had another idea: he would get his mother to help. "She's got an Argo and a quad," he said. "I think we can get them across the pond and right here to him. It'll take about four hours to go get them, though."

"You go ahead, and I'll stay right here and get this bull skinned," I said.

"We're a long way from nowhere," McInnis said. "I'm really not supposed to leave a client out here alone like that."

"I've got my pack and gun and everything I need to start a fire and stay the night if I had to," I said. "Plus, a shitload of moose to eat. If we wait to skin him, it'll be midnight before we get back. You go ahead. I'll have this sucker quartered up by the time you're back."

He smiled, reluctantly, and then turned and left me alone in the North Woods with my bull. I made the first cut on the point of the shoulder and parted the thick hide down the back of the front leg. I broke two Havalon blades and strained an ass muscle removing that first quarter, which weighed as much as a whitetail doe. But slowly, I took the moose apart. A shoulder, then a ham. Massive ball-and-socket joints. A 5-foot backstrap. I took a break, lying flat in the snow to relieve my muscles from the stooping and straining. That's when I noticed the ravens, circling and cawing overhead. I thought of wolves. Quiet as the North Woods seem, a kill is no secret. I got back to work and made sure my rifle was within reach.

I wedged a 10-inch log under the bull's spine, grabbed the opposite back leg by the ankle, and started rocking to flip him over. I don't know that I've ever asked any more of my muscles. I was screaming expletives when the moose finally gained enough momentum to roll. It hit with a thud, and I fell flat on my back—wheezing, dripping sweat, and caked in blood and mud. I peeled off all but a long-underwear shirt and continued cutting. As I was finishing the other front shoulder, the final quarter, I heard machines in the distance.

McInnis's mother, Nora Huggard, a petite lady, led the way with a chain saw bungeed to the quad's front rack. McInnis drove the amphibious Argo behind her. She walked toward me and grabbed the front leg to help. "Don't miss the neck meat," she said. "It's a good roast."

"I thought you said you'd have this thing skinned and done!" McInnis laughed, lighting a cigarette.

"Yeah, well you said it'd take you four hours, and it's only been three and a half!" I said back. "And by God, I'm down to the last shoulder."

We carefully wrapped the meat in game bags, hoisted them into the Argo's tiny bed, and took off, McInnis driving the Argo, me riding shotgun, and Nora behind us on the four-wheeler. He hit the beaver pond at full throttle, and the rear load nearly swamped us. With an inch of freeboard in the back and the front wheels kicking spray, I sprawled myself across the Argo's hood to keep the machine from sinking while McInnis got out and slogged through icy, waist-deep water to secure the winch cable to a spruce. I worked the winch switch with one hand and the steering bar with the other. We came to a stop next to the Jeep's tracks on the other side and then turned to look at Nora.

Balanced on her knees on the quad's gas tank, she plowed into the pond. McInnis was screaming, "Give it hell, Ma!," and hell is precisely what she gave. The back wheels disappeared under the murky water, but the front ones spun on the surface like paddle wheels. Steam boiled off the engine when she came to a stop on the other side, but she was almost perfectly dry.

"Honey, you're soaked," she said to her son. He lit a cigarette, and I could tell it was a struggle for her not to get after him. She was, after all, his mother.

From me, for the help, Nora would accept nothing more than a moose roast and a hug.

It was dark by the time we returned to camp—10 hours since I had pulled the trigger. As they say about moose hunting, the work doesn't begin until after the shot. That night, before bed, I took one last look at the quarters hanging from hooks in the side shed and admired the bull's paddles. What a trophy. I took some aspirin but couldn't sleep off the day's pain. Sometimes, I'd rather hurt than sleep.

Bo Whoop Comes Home

The mallards caught us at midmorning, when our guts were growling and our guard was down. Typical of late-season ducks, the pair was within gun range before anyone noticed them. Someone in the blind hissed "ducks" with the urgent tone that voids all gentlemen's rules of calling the shot. I grabbed and shouldered the gun leaning up next to me. It wasn't your typical duck gun. It was a big double, a 90-year-old HE-grade Super Fox with stamped barrels. The right one read MADE FOR NASH BUCKINGHAM; the left, BY BURT BECKER PHILA, PA. I pulled the front trigger, and the gun's report rippled through the green cypress and button willows. From the blind, it sounded like any other 12-gauge. But the guys at camp a quarter mile away later said they heard something different—a distinct, two-note report that they swore sounded just like it did in the legends: *bo-whoop*.

Tunica County, Mississippi, has changed a lot since Nash Buckingham's day. U.S. Highway 61 South long ago replaced the railroad and Limb Dodger as the primary mode of transportation for sportsmen traveling from Memphis to Tunica. The thickets full of quail are mostly gone, replaced by laser-leveled cotton and soybean fields. A strip of failing casinos sits on the banks of the Mississippi River, skeletons of promised economic progress in a region that consistently ranks among the country's poorest. Yet, the iconic Blue and White Restaurant is still there. It still opens before sunup, and it's still where many duck hunters like to eat breakfast, just as Buckingham did. And if you jump in a boat and motor a few hundred yards into the cypress trees of Beaver Dam Lake, you'll see a world that hasn't changed since Buckingham's day—a world the ducks still haunt every winter.

Most Southern duck hunters know something of Buckingham, arguably the most celebrated wing-shooting writer in history. His adventures were immortalized in seven books—most famously

De Shootinest Gent'man and Other Tales—and countless articles, including many in *Field & Stream*, where Buckingham was a regular contributor and, for a short stint, associate editor.

Yet, perhaps more famous than the man himself is his gun—the double-barrel Super Fox nicknamed Bo Whoop due to the sound of its report at a distance. Bo Whoop was built by renowned gunsmith Burt Becker, choked Full and Full, and it was designed for the hot new duck load of the day, Western Cartridge Co.'s Super-X 3-inch load of No. 4 lead shot. With that shell, Bo Whoop reportedly produced a 90 percent pattern at 40 yards, and Buckingham's ability to hit the "high birds," as he described them, with the combo was legendary. Bo Whoop was a key character in many of his stories.

Then, in 1948, after a morning of hunting in Arkansas, Bo Whoop was lost. As the story goes, Buckingham and his friend Clifford Green were checked by a couple of game wardens, one of whom asked to see the famous "big gun." Buckingham obliged, and at some point, the gun was set on the car fender. The hunters and officers then parted ways, and only after Buckingham and Green had driven a few miles down the road did they realize they'd left the gun on the fender. By the time they returned to get it, Bo Whoop was gone. Buckingham would never see his gun again.

The mystery of the gun's disappearance only fueled its legend and bolstered Bo Whoop's fame. Speculation and rumors surrounded its whereabouts for years. We do know that it was "found" in 2005, when an anonymous owner carried it into Darlington Gun Works in South Carolina to commission a replacement stock for the cracked original. The shop's owner, Jim Kelly, recognized the gun for what it was and contacted a historian with A.H. Fox, who verified it. Kelly told the owner what he had and offered $20,000 for the gun on the spot. The owner declined, and Kelly replaced the stock.

A few years later, the owner put the gun up for auction, and Bo Whoop was purchased for $201,250, including auction fees, by

Hal Howard Jr., Buckingham's godson. Howard then donated the gun to Ducks Unlimited (DU), and it's been on display at DU's national headquarters in Memphis, Buckingham's hometown, since 2010. The only better place for the gun to be is in a duck blind—which gave me an idea. I called a friend at DU and said what a story it would be if we took Bo Whoop back to Beaver Dam Lake for a hunt. After some discussion, the DU staff decided that's just what Buckingham would've wanted.

Reality began to set in once we were planning the hunt: I'd be the first writer since Buckingham to shoot Bo Whoop since it was lost—and I'd be shooting on Buckingham's home lake to boot. One night I had a dream that I dropped the gun—with a value higher than my house—into the mud. I felt more than a little pressure to kill a duck with it, too.

Before we actually hunted with Bo Whoop, the big gun's condition had to be evaluated by a gunsmith. After all, Buckingham fired a lot of magnum loads through it; that, and the gun was 90 years old. The DU staff took it back to Jim Kelly, who inspected the gun and deemed it mechanically sound. Because the old lead load for which Bo Whoop was designed isn't a legal option these days for duck hunting, we opted for a 2¾-inch, 1¼-ounce load of Kent Tungsten Matrix No. 5s, a safe alternative to steel shot in antique double guns.

With the gun no longer a safety concern, we got serious about the hunt. It would take place in late January, near the end of the 2015–2016 Mississippi duck season. Mike and Lamar Boyd, the father-and-son staff of Beaver Dam Hunting Services, would be our hosts. Their primary blind was in the Clover Leaf Hole, a large brake in the ancient cypress trees that was referenced on occasion in Buckingham's writings about Beaver Dam. DU's Dale Hall, Steve Maritz, Rogers Hoyt, and Hunter Shepard would be hunting with me as well. We just needed cooperative ducks.

The morning was mostly clear and cold with a stiff breeze. The gray ducks were stirring early, and within minutes of legal light, two of them set wings and dropped into the decoys. Maritz shouldered Bo Whoop and knocked them both down. It was fitting not only because gadwalls are a staple duck in sleepy Southern cypress brakes but also because it was a clean double. Buckingham wrote many things about Bo Whoop—but he rarely mentioned missing. Maritz passed the big gun to Hoyt, who didn't hold it long before three more gadwalls bombed the spread. He killed two of the birds with his first barrel, and he followed the third as it scrambled skyward. When the gadwall was about treetop high, the gun roared again, and the third duck plopped into the water.

"No misses in that gun!" Hoyt said.

He cracked the breech and handed the gun to me. I fished two shells from the open box and closed the gun with a crisp click. Bo Whoop lacks a mechanical safety, a feature Buckingham rejected because, as he saw it, a safety bred carelessness. I can tell you that the lack of one agitates restless nerves. I held the gun at low ready, barrels pointed outside the blind, waiting for my opportunity.

My first chance was at a white-fronted goose. Lamar worked the bird for several passes before I finally took a high overhead shot, some 50 yards up. The goose wilted but kept moving, so I fired the second barrel. The bird sailed into the timber behind the blind and required a couple of follow-up shots. It wasn't the cleanest kill, but it was a high bird with Bo Whoop and a gorgeous speck at that. I popped the smoking hulls out of the gun—keepsakes—and admired the black barring on the goose's chest. I sipped coffee with trembling hands.

The gun was passed on to the next man. I've hunted with skilled shooters in every flyway, most of them armed with synthetic-stocked autoloaders. I don't know that I've ever seen ducks killed with more efficiency than they were with Bo Whoop. Mike and Lamar each dropped gadwalls with single barrels. Before long, we were just duck hunting, taking turns shooting, laughing, and having a hell of a time. My anxiety over the $200,000 piece faded, replaced with the more familiar don't-miss-in-front-of-your-buddies pressure.

Perhaps it was that pressure that made each of us concentrate all the more carefully on not missing. Perhaps we were experiencing firsthand the capabilities of a custom-built piece from a bygone era of craftsmanship. Or perhaps the gun was magic. Regardless, I watched six men of different builds and experiences, men who've never before fired Bo Whoop at so much as a tin can, pick it up and mechanically drop one duck after another. No one got too spiritual, but all of us leaned toward magic.

Dale Hall, the CEO of DU, was adamant that everyone in the blind get a bird with Bo Whoop before he picked it up himself. By late morning, he was finally holding the gun but scanning empty skies. The hot flight had slowed to a trickle.

After two hours, Hall rested the big gun against a barrel rack in the Boyds' blind and stepped down into the boat hide for a quick break. That's when the two mallards dropped in. They were 30 yards out when we saw them, and when I shouldered Bo Whoop, the drake was closer still, backpedaling and oblivious. A man could not ask for a more perfect duck, and I did not want to disappoint the ghost of Nash Buckingham by missing. I pressed the front trigger. *Bo-whoop*. The greenhead fell with a splash, an orange leg kicking. I had another barrel left, but I let the hen fly out without using it.

There was little to explain, what with the smoking hull in one hand and dead greenhead in the other: I'd just killed Hall's duck. He only smiled and shook my hand; there was a light bloodstain around my thumbnail. "That is a beautiful bird," he said.

Buckingham wrote a lot about good guns and great shooting, but a more frequent theme was good company. That we have good company there seemed to make all the difference in our success. My duck heralded a flurry of late-morning mallards, and a few minutes later, Hall shot a greenhead of his own with Bo Whoop.

> *As we glide through weaving aisles I calculate that I have dropped ducks on well-nigh every square yard of this time-worn shooting ground. We have shared—still share—glorious years. The two of us are still hard at it. The reason? Because it has been left as it was. Because of sporting unselfishness and pride in its maintenance.* —Nash Buckingham, "What Rarer Day," Field & Stream, *November 1931*

To a nonhunter, it might seem strange that a tool so notoriously lethal on ducks is so closely tied to one of the earliest advocates of waterfowl conservation. Buckingham told great stories, but more than that, he used his platforms and voice to speak out against unregulated hunting and habitat destruction at a time when they presented a virtually unopposed threat to the resource. He's owed no small credit for the conservation awakening of the early 1900s that led to such notable things as the Migratory Bird Hunting Stamp Act and the founding of DU.

Of course, what a shotgun can represent for conservation makes perfect sense to a duck hunter. Because of sporting unselfishness and pride in maintenance, there are still mallards to be found on Southern cypress brakes like those on Beaver Dam Lake—and, for that matter, healthy numbers of ducks to be hunted and enjoyed in every flyway. There are still friendships to be made in blinds. There are still a few great old guns around to help tell the stories of then and now.

REDEMPTION BULL

Miles used to guide with Travis Reed, owner of Western Sky Outfitters in southern Colorado, and for a fee they'd treat you to a week of misery in the San Juan Mountains. There were no showers and only restless tent sleep. You'd burn so many calories each day that you'd eat about anything when you got back to camp, which may be why the highest praise I ever heard about the food there was that "it'll make a turd."

Their hunting camp was not for everyone. But in September, it sat in some of the finest elk country anywhere, all public land but not pressured much because you really needed horses and mules to pack the 10 miles in.

For many years, I had a rough go at elk hunting. I drew a cow tag once for eastern Kentucky and spent a couple of weeks floundering around trying to fill it. I never came close. I didn't get one in Idaho, where we rode a train of farting mules into the mountains each morning before daybreak, glassed empty hillsides all day, and then rode the mules back down in the dark, still farting even though they'd had all day to get it worked out. In New Mexico, there were elk everywhere, but that didn't make a difference for my luck. On the last morning before we left camp, I got to take a picture of all my friends smiling with their trophy elk racks. I was the perfect cameraman since I was the only person in camp that week who didn't shoot a bull.

In all of my trips, the closest I'd ever come to killing an elk was in a drainage near Western Sky's Colorado camp. I was hunting on an over-the-counter archery tag, back when those were available, and Miles was guiding me. I drew my bow on two different bulls that he called up during the week, but I didn't get a shot at either of them. It haunted me. After that, whenever I imagined a bugling elk, I always saw it standing among the white aspens in that very spot. I didn't want to just kill my first elk. I wanted to kill my first elk right there, in September.

After a two-year wait, I found myself back within walking distance of that drainage, with a muzzleloader tag that I'd applied for and drawn. The forecast promised a crisp opening morning. I had just one more hurdle to clear: the drainage is Miles's favorite spot, one he'd shown me, and he had two other hunters to guide. I was on a drop-camp hunt myself, which meant I'd be hunting alone and only in an area where Miles wasn't planning to guide someone else.

We were in the main wall tent with the cookstove, and Miles was picking his teeth with a pocketknife while I looked at him as if awaiting word from a prophet. "Brantley, you redneck son of a bitch," he finally said, "if you wander around in the dark long enough, do you think you can find that drainage where you scared all those bulls off a few years ago?"

It was all I could do not to leap from the table and start hiking up there that very moment, but I collected myself. "Oh, if you want to send me to that gar hole again, I guess that'd be okay."

I was in elk as soon as shooting light broke. After a couple of hours, I had close calls on two bulls. When a third one bugled from deep within the drainage, I checked the wind and scrambled over the break of the ridge. I could see the open slope on the opposite side, and I was pretty sure that's where the bull was. It wasn't the best place to set up, but it was the best I had. I backed up 50 yards, took a seat next to an aspen, propped the open-sighted muzzleloader on my knee as if I were turkey hunting, and made a "might-as-well-try" mew on an open-reed cow call.

The last thing I expected was for the bull to launch himself into a bugling frenzy, growling as he charged down the opposite hillside and up the ridge right to me. But that's just what he did. He even loped to a broadside stop 30 yards away. I had the hammer cocked and the sights aligned on the crease of his shoulder.

The smoke lingered a minute over the drainage, and I went to sit next to my first elk, just to look at him a while. It was only after I'd gutted the bull and shouldered my pack that I looked around and realized I was standing in the very place where, for years, I'd been envisioning that very moment. I pulled out my GPS and dropped a waypoint so we could bring the horses to him, and I sent an inReach message to Miles and Michelle: bull down!

Even with the horses, we knew it'd be an all-day job getting my elk out. On a peak above the drainage, Miles and I dismounted and led the horses into the vertical hell below, where it was too dangerous to sit in a saddle. On some of the peaks there, there's enough cell service to check in. Miles declared that he had one bar and stared at his phone. Then he looked at me and said, "I might have to kill your wife."

Michelle had shared a screenshot of my earlier inReach message on Facebook with a post that said, "Somewhere on a mountain, among those trees, the hubby is quartering and packing out an elk." It was innocent enough, except that the whole purpose of an inReach message is to show a map of exactly where the sender is—which in that case was in the middle of public elk nirvana.

I had a satellite phone in my pack, and I'd told Michelle that I'd be using it only for emergencies. When I dialed her up at work, she answered in a panic until I grilled her about the Facebook post. Miles was leaning over his saddle horn, eavesdropping intently.

"What I ought to do is slap the shit out of you both," she said. "Look at the post again and give me a little credit. I cropped out the coordinates before I posted it. And by the way, congrats on your first elk. It took you long enough."

It was nearly dark before we were back at camp, my elk quarters hung up in game bags and covered in pine boughs. Slabs of backstrap steak were sizzling in butter, and there was enough to share with everyone. "That'll make a better turd than usual," Miles said when I handed him a plate. "So, you like my elk spot?"

"Miles, I've traveled the country for elk, and that might be the best gar hole I've hunted," I said. "I'm glad the entire world doesn't know where it is."

Tahr Camp

There was chunk of chamois meat stuck to the outside of the tent. David Draper was sitting in a damp chair, snapping twigs and trying to rekindle our small fire, but he'd been waiting since first light to show someone the piece of flesh.

"Like a bunch of damned savages," I said. Draper nodded and smiled. I looked at my boots and wondered for a second if they could be dry. They weren't. I pulled off my socks, the last dry pair I had, and pressed my bare feet into the cold, soggy soles. "I'm going to get water for coffee," I said and walked to the river.

The quiet is eerie in New Zealand. It's one of the first things I noticed about the place. There are few birds or even insects. No coyotes to howl or bears to consider. It is, in a word, foreign.

And yet, it's a mountain hunter's paradise. We chartered a helicopter to get to the level spot, where we made camp. The chopper landed in the valley only long enough for us to throw out our tents, cooking gear, and a case of Speight's, and then we hustled back inside, and within a couple minutes, we'd been ferried up to a saddle between two mountain peaks and left behind. Below was a drainage that snaked through five miles of rugged country to its confluence with the river, next to our camp. We'd be hunting wild chamois, and five miles didn't seem like much.

New Zealand has a rich and diverse hunting culture. The duck opener could be a national holiday. There's a lot of high-fenced red stag shooting, too. But we weren't there for either of those. Like a variety of big-game species, chamois were released onto the South Island in the early 1900s, and with a lack of natural predators, they thrived in the Southern Alps. Our guide, Dan Rossiter, enjoyed hunting them over everything else.

During his off time—he builds houses when he's not guiding—Dan likes to spend a few days hiking into and camping in remote areas, chasing those dainty, 80-pound animals. We had only a couple days there before being bound for a different area—to hunt tahr—and just walking in would've burned up all of our time. So, we cheated a little on the front end by having the chopper drop us into some of Dan's favorite country.

We could still hear the hum of the helicopter as we sat down on the saddle to glass. It was big country but deceptive, not nearly as open on the ground as it seemed from above. The greenery along the drainages was head-high and rainforest-dense. Still, after an hour, I picked out a lone chamois buck a thousand or more yards away.

"That's a good one, mate," Dan said, looking over the critter himself. "We should get closer."

We began picking our way down the mountainside. Dan led the way, followed by Scott Olmstead, editor in chief of *American Hunter*, and Draper, editor of *Petersen's Hunting*. Dan suddenly motioned for us to "stop and get down."

Three buck chamois previously unseen by us were feeding on a grassy flat 300 yards below. None of them were especially big, but out there, Dan said, you take what you get. We liked the prospect of fresh chamois backstrap over freeze-dried Chili-Mac, too. We rested our rifles on packs, counted down from three, and commenced shooting. All three bucks fell dead within sight. It took longer to hike to them than to spot them, set up, and shoot them.

We ate lunch after taking pictures and before wielding our knives. Then we set to work, cutting the chamois up and arranging quarters and skulls into our packs. All we had to do, it seemed, was walk back to camp, have us a hell of a meal, and call for the chopper a day early.

Kiwi Dan was a badass, with understated confidence. As we hiked back toward camp, I'd catch glimpses of him ahead, sitting and patiently waiting on the three Americans behind him to catch up. I'm not sure that I saw him take more than a deep breath. The incline wasn't of a straight-down, fall-and-you're-dead grade, but close. Dan walked across it like tile floor. My pack was heavy with meat (though not as heavy as Dan's), and so I descended the slopes by zigzagging across them, back and forth, gradually losing altitude, but never daring to straighten my legs for fear of hyper-extending a knee. If you're a sea-level guy like me, I don't care how many miles you run, weights you lift, or workout stories you create on Instagram. A lean mountain hunter like Dan, born and raised in country, will be tougher and faster.

We were less than a mile down the drainage, sweating pretty good, when a buck chamois suddenly stood up from behind a lone boulder just 30 yards away. Probably, it was the same buck we'd spotted from a thousand yards above earlier that morning. Dan hissed to shoot, and Draper killed it before any of us really thought it through.

"Best day of wild chamois hunting you're ever going to see, mates," Dan said as he quartered the animal. Then he paused. "We have a bad spot up ahead. A wee bit of brush. It takes about 45 minutes to get through it. We'd best not shoot any more chamois."

The brush was a conifer of some sort. Most of it was about 7 feet tall, and because of the grade, it grew perpendicular to us as much as it grew upward. Its limbs were woven tight as a net, and we'd step from one mass of it to the next, hanging on to limbs above us and praying that the ones below us wouldn't give way. Olmstead tore loose a muscle in his ribs—his doctor confirmed it later—and we were all gouged and bloodied. During a short break, I watched Dan check the footing on a bush below him. He smiled, took a step forward, and disappeared from sight. I clawed my way toward him, and where he'd disappeared was a chute the diameter of a man, 75 yards long and spilling out into the white-water creek below.

"Dan?!" I yelled. I couldn't have heard him over the torrent if he answered. I heard Draper picking his way through the brush above me.

"Brantley, I can't see a damn thing. Which way?" he yelled.

"Not this way. It's bad," I replied, not quite ready to reveal that Dan had disappeared before my eyes. I saw a flash of movement at the bottom of the chute. Dan leaned in from the bottom, smiled, and motioned for me to come on. I turned to Draper. "Never mind! Come on this way!"

I'd call it a controlled fall, sliding through the chute with my rifle across my chest, grabbing limbs above me to slow the descent. At the bottom, Dan said, "We can pretty well follow the creek the rest of the way. One time I tried hiking down the other side to get to here. That was a real pain in the ass."

We soaked our boots during the final half mile to camp, where the creek began to settle into the river with wider, deeper pools. The sun was setting when we reached the valley. Dan began setting tents as Draper fished through cooking utensils. Olmstead and I gathered armloads of firewood and began arranging backstraps into the grass before us.

"Three of them ought to be a good start, right?" I asked. He nodded. An assembly line of sorts was formed around the fire: meat, seasonings, butter and skillet, flask of whiskey. We worked by light of headlamps. Olmstead sliced, Draper seasoned, and I fried. Dan fed butter to the skillet and manned a plate of cooked meat. Occasionally, he'd pass around beers. The flask never lingered in one place for long. We drained it in short order and so retrieved a second one.

We sipped red wine off the threads between dripping mouths full of chamois meat. At some point, Draper hauled three more backstraps to the circle, one of which he cut in half and simply tossed into the coals of our fire. We scraped off the ash 15 minutes later and ate slices of it off the blades of our pocketknives.

Maybe the next day, we'd eat a vegetable. But that night was for fire and meat and blades, befit for a bunch of damned savages. No one howled at the moon, but I think we all considered it.

Making coffee with river water, next to Draper's new fire, I was a little sad to hear the helicopter humming our way—but excited to see what a tahr hunt was all about.

Tahr camp was a sheepherder's hut lined with a dozen bunks and dusty linens but without power or running water. We arrived just before dark the night before, joined by young assistant guide Bre Lewis, with the quarters and cape of a good 12-inch bull tahr already in tow. We'd spotted him on the drive in, and Olmstead killed him after a short stalk.

Himalayan tahr are heavy, goat-like animals four times the size of a chamois. Both sexes have horns, but a good bull's will measure 12 inches plus and be thick as a man's forearm. In the winter, bulls develop magnificent manes. Like chamois, tahr were introduced to New Zealand. Although they're listed as threatened in much of their true home range, they're so numerous in areas of the South Island that government sharpshooters are employed to control them. But for the most part, hunters manage their numbers.

It was February, early fall there, and at that time of the season, small herds of tahr spend their middays loafing and resting in high-elevation areas but move down to grassy benches late in the evening to feed. Driving in the night before after Olmstead killed his bull, we saw two good bulls feeding right in the valley, which Dan said almost never happens. "Mostly, if you want to kill a bull tahr, you're going to have to climb for him," he said.

I did want to climb. There was a flurry of movement for the first hour the next morning, but as the sun rose, the tahr in the easy-to-reach areas seemed to vanish. Dan stopped the truck on a warm flat alongside the river just before noon, and we shuffled around from glassing to picking at lunch to dozing on our packs. I was nodding off when, from behind a spotting scope, Dan said, "Check this one out, Mate."

The bull was bedded on the mountainside across the valley a mile away, with 15 females. He was a nice one, probably a 12-incher, Dan said, but he had an especially thick mane for that early in the season. Best of all, he was bedded at the edge of a tree line, and I liked the idea of sneaking in close to him.

We crossed the valley in Dan's truck and then Dan, Bre, and I slipped into the timber below the herd. It was the first scope of big woods I'd seen, and the understory was soft and quiet. We moved quickly up the face, stopping at a bubbling creek to fill our canteens. "I reckon we've got a good chance of killing this bull," Dan said. We hustled another hundred yards uphill before taking to our knees and crawling out into the meadow. We were 100 yards from where we'd last seen the bull from the valley, and at first, it seemed the herd had disappeared. But suddenly, a single nanny appeared from behind an unseen fold in the terrain above us. The rest of the herd strolled out single file, walking right to us. Dan hissed for me to shoot, but the bull was in the back, and I could see only the top of its head. Finally, I shouldered my rifle, a Savage .30-06, and sat up just high enough to see to the base of the bull's neck and top of his chest. That was enough. A single bullet dropped him where he stood.

It is true that New Zealand is a foreign place to me. But the sounds of happy hunters with knives at work and quarters being lashed to packs was universal. I felt right at home.

First Sit

Looking at the 8-pointer I'd missed not an hour earlier, I felt good about my decision to be such a bow snob. I'd almost grabbed a crossbow before going out that morning, and had I done that, I'd have killed that buck less than five minutes into the new day. Instead, I'd brought my compound, misjudged the distance by 10 yards, and sailed one right under his belly.

Because I'd missed, I was still in the tree when a far bigger 8 chased a doe to 75 yards. They stopped in a patch of honeysuckle, where I could see the buck's tines flashing in the sunlight. That's when the one I'd missed reappeared and eased toward the thicket, one cautious step at a time, as if he knew better but couldn't help himself. The big buck burst from the honeysuckle, ears pinned, and rammed the smaller one in the ribs, thrashing him into the dirt and then chasing him out of sight. But not out of earshot. The next five minutes were a cacophony of violence; it sounded as if the big 8 had the smaller one stuck onto his antlers and was plowing a swath through the timber with him.

Meanwhile, the doe stepped out of the honeysuckle and began browsing casually on turnip greens. I knew her respite would be short-lived, though, because sure as the world turns, that big buck would be coming back to her. I clipped my release to my d-loop and waited.

Michelle and I had hung the stand in a poplar at the edge of the creek bank, near the old cabin, back in September. It was just upstream of where the footlog used to be and on the bend of a firebreak that's 15 yards wide and separates the creek from an overgrown field. Earlier that summer, when we were working on plots, Michelle pulled her tractor up to mine at the end of the day and shut it off. "Where you been?" I asked.

"Tilling up a spot along the firebreak near the creek, like we've been threatening to do for years," she said. "We're going to hunt that this season."

Michelle killed her buck in a different spot in early October, so when the rut rolled around, the creek-side stand remained untouched. I snuck in at noon on November 2 to check a trail camera that we'd set there when we planted the plot. What had been bare dirt was now an ankle-high oasis of turnips and oats. The camera showed a lone, long-faced doe that seemed to live there. I didn't see any daylight photos of big bucks, but my gut said to hunt it. I set my alarm early, paddled up the creek in the dark, and climbed into the tree.

It was a cup of coffee, as much as my poor shooting, that saved that smaller 8-pointer. I wasn't expecting to see a deer until the morning's frost burned off, and so instead of ranging things, I was pouring myself a cup when I saw him walking down the firebreak right to me. By the time I set down my coffee, the buck was in bow range. I looked at his rack and started to think, "Boy, he'd be a nice one next year" as I hit full draw. Too late. After I missed him clean, he bounded, white flag up, into the honeysuckle thicket.

I smiled, nocked another arrow, and freshened my cold cup of coffee. The sun had just burned away the frost when I heard the grunts and watched the doe prance out of the thicket. The buck boiled out from behind her, a beast of an animal that dwarfed the young one I'd just missed.

After chasing the smaller buck away, thrashing him from ridge to ridge, the big 8 seemed to be gone for good. But then I spotted his rack twisting left and right as he worked a licking branch on the far side of the honeysuckle. The doe was just 50 yards from me and working closer when he rushed at her. She skipped down a trail and stopped broadside in the plot, in chip-shot range. As soon as his nose hit that trail, I drew—and just as I bleated to stop him, the same smaller 8-pointer burst out of the fallow field and ran right at them, like some brat cannonballing into the city pool. Deer scattered. Within seconds, the bucks were 100 yards away, with me still at full draw.

I let down, scanned for the doe, and found her under my stand, peering into the creek at the open bow case in my johnboat. "It's all over," I thought.

But then she looked back toward the firebreak, snorted, and took off. The big 8 was bearing down fast, his legs loose as leather strops. I yanked my bow back again and yelled a bleat at him as he ran under the stand, and he stopped, slightly quartering away, at five steps. I touched the release, the arrow buried into his heart, and he ran a frantic half circle and fell dead 30 yards away.

I sat down. It occurred to me, after all of that coffee, that I needed to pee, but damned if I could balance on my knocking knees. So, I held it and watched. The doe stood at one end of the firebreak, stamping her foot before taking off again. The smaller 8 swung around the plot and chased her up into the timber.

I was in no hurry to climb down. You only get a first sit once.

The Tiniest Buck I Ever Hunted

I probably should've shot the first buck I saw. My buddy Justin Moore and I were hiking down a switchback trail on a western Oregon hillside, through prime blacktail country, but with our attention focused on the little whitetails skittering in the valley below us. A fence-line thicket and a 100-yard-wide buffer of oaks separated the hillside we were on from a small housing subdivision. There were miles of wild country all around, but in classic whitetail fashion, most of the deer we saw seemed to prefer life on the fringes of backyards, where there were good gardens to pilfer and acorns fattened on fertilizer.

I first saw the 8-point in question as he strolled across a lawn, crossed behind an aboveground pool, and then meandered through the oaks. He jumped a low wire in the fence, lip-curled at a nearby doe, and then stopped to pluck blackberries from a withering vine.

Moore, a native Oregonian, whispered that it was a pretty good buck as Columbian whitetails go. I ranged the deer at 218 yards and was seated with my rifle on shooting sticks, and the buck was standing at a safe angle to shoot, relative to the houses. There was no good reason to pass the shot, really, except that it was only an hour into the first morning, and I wanted to keep hunting. We watched the buck feed on blackberries for 45 minutes and then bed at the base of the bush.

The tiny Columbian whitetail is the westernmost whitetail subspecies in the United States, native only to a few niche habitats in Oregon and Washington. Hunting opportunities for them are exceedingly limited. They were formerly listed as an endangered species but then delisted after populations recovered. Most of the modern populations are still under federal protection, but limited tags have been available since 2005 to hunt the Roseburg population, along the Umpqua River, about 75 miles south of Eugene. That's where we were. Even there, tags can take years to draw for the few controlled public-land hunts held in the area, but a handful of outfitters do secure limited private-land-only tags. We were hunting with Jody Smith, a well-known area outfitter who guides year-round for big game, spring turkeys, and the usual fish of the Northwest: smallmouth bass to salmon to sturgeon.

Coveted as a Columbian whitetail tag is and rare as we knew the deer to be, the critters in practice still acted just like the whitetails I'm used to hunting back home in Kentucky. And at least around the fencerows and oak hammocks bordering that subdivision, there were plenty of them. We saw does, fawns, and young bucks every trip out.

Smith shared some trail camera photos with us ahead of time and cautioned us to not expect to see a Midwestern- or even Southeastern-caliber whitetail on this hunt. A big Columbian buck might weigh 120 pounds on the hoof. While most big-game records organizations don't have a specific Columbian whitetail category, Safari Club International (SCI) does. The current SCI typical record scored 138⅜, and the nontypical measured 144⅛. Bucks eligible for entry into the SCI record books must score 70 inches and 80 inches for the typical and nontypical categories, respectively.

There were some good potential tree-stand and ground-blind locations near the fencerow, but we employed Western glassing and stalking tactics on these whitetails. It was perfect country for it, too. Smith drove Moore, David Draper, and me to the spine of a ridge just before daybreak, and from there we glassed and hunted our way down the hillside.

Later that first morning, looking over photos of the buck Moore had taken with a telephoto lens, Smith agreed that the deer was probably a shooter. Moore and I snuck back over the ridge early that afternoon and took a seat 150 yards above the blackberry bush, where we'd seen the buck bed earlier. I assumed the deer would stand and provide an easy shot sometime before dark; instead, we never saw him again.

We were socked in with fog the next morning, making for a slow sit, so we took a drive around the property at midday. The place looked like classic Pacific Coast wine country (or at least what I expect wine country should look like; my experience with wine is limited mostly to the stuff in boxes). Golden hillsides rolled into oak hammocks full of mature trees and virtually no understory. As we rounded a turn on the low side of one of the hammocks, a nice buck stood from his bed and trotted into the timber, half-heartedly waving his white flag, as if he were more annoyed than alarmed.

"There's a group of five bucks that have been bedding in there since September," Smith said. "A little sneak through there might not be a bad plan."

With that in mind, we made a wide circle back to the top of the ridge and worked ourselves into a good headwind. Draper dropped below a parallel hillside and snuck his way toward where we'd jumped the buck, figuring he might get a shot at anything I kicked out of the oaks. Moore and I stepped into the head of the oak hammock and began still-hunting our way through it, glassing more than walking. We didn't make it far before I spotted a buck 60 yards ahead, staring back at us. He flagged and trotted out of sight, and I saw additional deer trotting through the timber with him. I knew our wind was good and the deer hadn't seemed too spooked, and so I thought, as bedded whitetails sometimes do at home, these might circle back through the area, given a little time. We set our packs on the ground and stretched against them to wait.

It didn't take long. Within 10 minutes, Moore spotted a deer slipping through the trees below us. The bucks we'd jumped were just 70 yards away and walking toward us, alert, but not enough to ignore the acorns on the ground or sparring with one another.

I zoomed my scope to 10× and settled the crosshair on the biggest buck's shoulder but then hesitated; I hadn't taken a close look at him. I waited for him to turn his head, and I counted 8 tines, but thin ones. I flicked the safety off, looked at his shoulder again, touched the trigger, and then stopped myself. I watched him walk away through the scope. The circumstances tempted me to shoot, but the truth was, he was a much smaller buck than the one I'd passed the previous morning. I held fire.

Early afternoon found us back on the hillside overlooking the fencerow. I was glassing near the fence gap the buck had hopped through the first morning, and Draper was just over the hill, maybe 75 yards above me, glassing a different slope. Moore was standing between us, picking apart blackberry bushes with his spotting scope.

I looked up from my binoculars to see him motioning at me. He had a bachelor group of bucks in his spotter, including two nice 8-pointers. The best one was wide and pretty, but there was a tall, heavy buck in the mix, too. The deer were browsing on a flat 300 yards away, just below Draper. I could see him glassing the deer on the ridge above me. He motioned toward them, and I replied with a thumbs-up.

As the bucks were on Draper's side of the ridge, I didn't plan to shoot until after he shot first. But our rifles, Nosler M21s in 6.5 Creedmoor, were suppressed, and we were far enough away that I figured I'd get a decent opportunity if he made good on his first shot. I settled onto the hillside and began building my nest, with my pack braced against the incline behind me and my rifle's fore end clamped onto a tripod rest. I was using a Leupold rangefinding binocular, and it was the perfect tool for both watching the deer intently and keeping constant tabs on their distance. It looked like my shot, if it happened, would be about 270 yards, and so I dialed the scope accordingly and waited for the crack of Draper's rifle.

I heard the whump of a solid hit first, followed by the gun. Through my glass, the wide 8-pointer buckled and fell, and the other bucks scattered. I dropped the binos, found the tall buck in my scope, zoomed, and waited. He stalled in the brush for a moment before stepping into the open, broadside, and walking with determination back toward the fencerow thicket. I squeezed the trigger, and there was another whump at the shot. I knew I hit the buck hard, but when he hunched, walked a few steps, and bedded, I feared a liver hit. A follow-up shot through both shoulders put him down for good. We recovered both deer within 30 yards of one another.

Was the deer I shot as big as the one I passed the first day? I won't spend much time worrying about that. We set in to gutting our Columbian whitetails, tiny trophies that they were, with the sun setting over the Oregon countryside. Wine country, perhaps. Not too far in the distance, I could hear the sounds of a family barbecue, and I figured that probably somewhere close, a whitetail was eyeing a garden for dinner.

Fresh Beavers and Big Bears

I thought it would be a thrill to have a black bear climb into my tree stand with me, as they sometimes do on baited hunts. Then I watched a sow walk under the 15-foot-high wooden platform where I was sitting and look up. She clearly spotted me, but instead of scampering away, she stood on her hind legs, dug her front claws into the bark of my stand tree, and scaled 7 feet up almost instantly.

You'd think an animal as heavy as a black bear, even a smallish one, would shinny and fumble a bit while climbing a slick tree trunk, but the sow simply put one paw in front of the other and pulled herself up with no apparent effort at all. In the time it took for me to stand up and take a step back, she was level with my feet and close enough to slap on the nose. Not that I planned on slapping her on the nose.

"Git!" I yelled. But she only twisted her head slightly, as if to get a better look at me, and then climbed a little higher. Turns out, the novelty of having a bear that close is pretty fleeting, and I quickly reached for my rifle.

In northern Alberta, my friend Linda Powell told me the story of a hunter who sat back while a bear climbed the ladder of his stand. The bruin stopped at the guy's feet, eyed his boot laces for a bit, and then began gnawing on them. At that point, the hunter shot the bear out of the tree, filling the second of his two tags.

Powell, who works for Mossberg and who invited me on the trip, had been coming to Wally Mack's bear camp for years. Mack and his wife, Louisa, had been running the camp and guide service for 30 years. Their sons, Shawn and Kristen, helped them with the day-to-day guiding, and when I was there, Wally said the boys would take over completely in a few years.

In Wally's bear camp, running out of tags is a common problem. The area is crawling with bears, and the guides keep some 40 bait-and-stand sites running all spring, from May to mid-June. Most sites get a generous helping of fresh bait—oats soaked in fryer grease, marshmallows, gummy worms, cake icing—every two or three days. Hunters get two bear tags, and during a five-day hunt, most get the chance to hang them both on big bears.

My first opportunity came quickly, about a half hour into the first evening. A goliath bruin lumbered in from the bush and stood over the bait barrel 15 yards from me. I'd hunted bears a bit and knew the basic cues for judging a bear's size, but I'd never hunted the animals over bait and had never been so close to one. So, I watched him for a bit.

The bear seemed to check all the boxes of being a mature boar. He was taller at the shoulders than the 55-gallon drum full of bait, and you certainly couldn't stuff him inside that barrel—Wally's number-one tip for field-judging bears. "If it seems like a bear could fit inside the bait barrel, it's too small," he told us before the hunt.

But even without the barrel for reference, this bear looked big. His head was round, with a deep dimple between the eyes. I knew for sure he was a shooter when he stood and bit into the beaver carcass that was suspended from a log, 7 feet up in the air.

The Macks purchased skinned beaver carcasses from local trappers. Kristen, my guide for the week, said that a good day of bear hunting starts with a fresh beaver. The rancid ones that have been riding in the bait refill bucket for a while attract bears just as well, but handling them is no fun at all. The guides chop the beaver carcasses in half with an ax and then take a half portion in with them when they drop hunters off in the stand, securing it by rope while the hunter gets settled.

Powell was the one who told me that the dangling beaver carcass is a good reference of a bear's length. Any bear that can stand on its hind legs and reach it easily is more than 6 feet long, and one you should consider shooting. When that first bear I saw stood and simply bit into the dangling beaver, audibly crushing bone and causing a gob of entrails to slither out onto his face and then sag to the ground with a plop, I knew for sure he was big. I shouldered my rifle, a Mossberg Patriot in 7 PRC, and killed him right there. He measured 7 feet 9 inches—an immense black bear anywhere they're found.

My second bear walked in two evenings later, and even from 100 yards out, I knew he was big. A small bear was already on the bait, and it bolted as the big boar approached, swaggering left and right, a full half shoulder taller than the bait barrel. I'd been calm with the first bear, and the decision to shoot was almost clinical. With the second one, I had to calm my breathing and force myself to hold the crosshairs tight on his vitals. But the shot was good. The bear lurched into the brush and was dead within 20 yards. I texted Kristen, told him I was tagged out, and began gathering my stuff to climb down and have a look at my trophy.

I was halfway down the ladder when I looked over my shoulder and saw that the smaller bear was back on the bait. So, I climbed back up to wait, and that's when I noticed the sow approaching, walking along the same path that the big boar had used. She'd obviously seen me moving and was now closing in fast to the base of my stand.

Kristen had told me that moving around when bears are close can actually attract them, and even trigger a territorial response. "Bears climb trees when they're afraid," he said, "and when they see you up there, they think you're another bear that's afraid of them. The ones with an attitude will climb the tree to mess with you."

I wasn't really afraid of the sow attacking me; I did, after all, have a high-powered rifle leveled at her face. But I was out of bear tags and couldn't legally shoot, except in self-defense. I wasn't entirely sure where that defensive threshold was, and I didn't care to explain the situation to a wildlife officer after the fact.

I hit record on the camera of my phone and held it in one hand—my rifle in the other—to document events just in case. I jabbed at the bear's face with the muzzle and yelled for it to "Get down!" But even being poked with my rifle barrel didn't seem to bother the sow much, and my thoughts turned to the live cartridge in the chamber and my thumb resting against the safety. Was I going to have to shoot this bear?

I shouted louder and more urgently. The sow looked around as if she were bored and then, finally, shuffled back down the tree. She rushed at the smaller bear that was on the bait, slapped the drum full of oiled oats in an attempt to knock it over, and began eating, which is when I heard the sound of Kristen's 4-wheeler approaching.

"I've got a big one down right over there in the bush, and I had a smaller one try to eat me!" I said. We wrestled my boar, another trophy at 7 feet 5 inches, onto the rack of Kristen's 4-wheeler. Then I showed him the video of the sow on my phone. He chuckled and said, "Yep, that one was close, eh?"

In the end, having not been eaten, I'd say it was kind of a thrill having a bear climb into the stand with me—just not as much of a thrill as hearing Kristen's 4-wheeler coming in to pick me up.

Elk Don't Gobble

One of the surest ways to upset a Western hunter is to tell him that elk hunting is "just like turkey hunting." I've seen some Westerners become visibly upset over such a declaration—fighting mad, even—as they explain how chasing a majestic, 700-pound Rocky Mountain bull in no way compares to hunting a stupid, 20-pound bird.

Of course, when they say such things, I like to turn up the Southern drawl and remind them that I'm not referring to the Merriam's turkeys they're accustomed to hunting out West. Obviously, just about anybody can call one of those in. No, what I'm saying is that elk hunting is a lot like hunting *eastern* wild turkeys, except that it's a little easier.

Do I actually have to believe that? No, of course not. Elk hunting probably is more challenging, on average, than turkey hunting. But stirring up shit around the campfire is a uniquely good time, at least to me. And besides, anyone who claims that elk hunting and turkey hunting have nothing in common just hasn't done enough of both of them. Maybe they're not just alike but by golly, they're pretty close.

Of course, that comes with some qualifiers. Late-season elk hunting—and all of the walking and glassing it usually requires—is only a little more entertaining to me than working on my taxes. Meanwhile, I do enjoy fall turkey hunting, but when I shoot a gobbler in October, I feel as if I've cheated myself out of something really good for the following spring. So, in general, I avoid it.

What I'm comparing is September elk hunting to April turkey hunting. It's partly the calling that makes them so similar, but it's even more so the maneuvering, strategy, and woodsmanship. Because I grew up chasing gobblers in the hills and hollers of Kentucky and Tennessee and because I love it only slightly less than I love my own family, it stands to reason that I also very much enjoy hunting rutting elk in September.

And so, I was in a fine mood indeed in the predawn of September 12 as we hiked to a peak that would be a good vantage for overlooking a Utah sage flat. All of my September elk hunting previous to that had been on public land in Colorado with a bow or open-sighted muzzleloader. I'd managed to kill a couple bulls doing that, which my Western hunting buddies described as "cute little rag horns."

But that morning, we were on the legendary Ensign Ranch, and I was experiencing elk hunting in a way that I knew I might never see again. I had a rifle in hand, bulls were bugling all around, and I knew some of them were big ones. I was there as a guest of Federal Ammunition to test out their new 7 mm Backcountry rifle cartridge and report the results. I've definitely had worse assignments.

Besides learning all I could about the new cartridge, I had two personal hunting goals in mind. One, I wanted to take a nice, mature bull back home to Kentucky. But more than that, I wanted to shoot a bull that came storming into the call, bugling, slobbering, and pissing himself. That, more than antler size, is what I crave out of an elk hunt.

My guide, Max Ahlstrom, thought we could probably check off both goals and find a big bull that would "act right." Despite being only in his early twenties, Max had been hunting and guiding for elk since his early teenage years, and the experience showed in his poise and confidence. We'd parked his truck in a low valley well before daybreak and hiked up to the peak, where we sat down to glass. The sage flat was across the drainage, and that's where we expected the elk to be.

We'd had a positively electric hunt there the evening before. It was warm and sunny to start out, and we'd began the afternoon with a relaxed, "go hunting and see what happens" sort of pace, cruising through peaks and valleys with the windows down, talking about life and stopping to glass on occasion. But matters suddenly became more urgent when Max spotted a big 6×6 bull milling on a ridge about a thousand yards away. "I believe that one's a sure shooter," he said. We backed the pickup out of sight, gathered our packs, and made our move.

We used the break of a hill to disappear into a stand of junipers, cross a fence, and sneak to the edge of a dirt road that snaked along the spine of the ridge toward the bull. Max checked the wind, and it was soft and in our face. I found a nice hide just ahead of him and rested my rifle on Trigger Sticks as he mewed with cow calls. Maybe it wasn't April in the dogwoods with a 12-gauge on my knee, but it didn't feel far from it. The bull clopped into the open up ahead, in view but out of range, then stretched his neck, and bugled. I thought I'd shoot him walking straight down the road toward us, and I began ranging rocks and trees for reference. But instead, one cow and then another trotted across the road, and the bull turned and followed them into the brush.

The hillside was thick and tangled, but it spilled into a green meadow below, and Max thought the herd would end up there before the end of shooting light. We backed into the cover ourselves and picked our way down the hillside until we were within 200 yards of the meadow. It was already alive with elk. A big 5-pointer was herding cows and bugling as he went, and a couple smaller satellite bulls were watching on the periphery like pimpled freshmen at a high school dance. I affixed my bipod to my rifle and settled in, resting the stock over my pack for a rock-solid prone position. A cow emerged from the brush, just below where we'd seen the big 6-pointer disappear. The shadows were getting long, but I thought I was just minutes away from a 200-yard shot at the bull in the meadow.

Instead, Max suddenly hissed, "He's up here!" Sure enough, he'd spotted the bull standing in a small opening within the junipers, raking its antlers against a bush. The bull was just a touch more than 400 yards away, well within range of the rifle and at a distance where I'd done some practicing. I grabbed my pack and rebuilt my rest, dialed my scope turret accordingly, held on the bull's shoulder—but then relaxed my trigger finger.

No doubt, the distance was the biggest reason. Four hundred yards is a long way. And too, the bull was surrounded by heavy cover. I knew I probably had one shot, and if the hit wasn't perfect, we'd have a long night on our hands. Besides that, I wanted to shoot a bull that we'd called to the gun. "I think you've got him right there," Max whispered, watching the animal through his spotting scope and waiting to see the bullet's impact. I could sense a hint of frustration from my guide at my lack of shooting—but the situation just wasn't right. I opened the bolt of my rifle, pressed the ejected cartridge down into the magazine, and closed the bolt again on the empty chamber.

"I think I could've had him, too—but I'm not taking that shot tonight," I whispered. "It's been one hell of an elk hunt, though."

Max found the same 6-pointer through his spotting scope just after daybreak. The bull was alone, best we could tell, slowly working its way across the sage flat toward a herd of cows that was being tended by the big 5-pointer from the evening before.

We shuffled down from the peak and hustled across the valley and then used a drainage to sneak our way up toward the sage flat while staying out of sight. A bull, probably the 5-pointer, bugled just above us and out of sight, and his cows chirped. Max and I squatted, knowing we were close enough to spoil the entire situation with a shifting wind but still out of position for killing the 6-pointer. "I think we go for it and keep moving up," he whispered.

We'd just crested the break of the hill and found cover behind a larger bush on the flat when we spied the 6-pointer 400 yards ahead. The smaller bull had moved his harem well off to our left, and so we were somewhat between them. "I bet you can call him in," I said. Max cow-called softly, and the big bull immediately spun our way, bugled, and began walking.

Max filmed it all through the lens of his spotting scope, and I saved the video to watch over and again. The excitement was palpable as the bull worked closer, with Max calling out the distance every few seconds. "He's at 300. 280. 240. 200. 175."

I was on my knees, resting the fore-end of the rifle across my Trigger Sticks, the scope turned to 8 power and the safety off. The bull was head-on and covering ground for a good stretch, but he finally had to turn to walk around a larger clump of bushes, putting him broadside for a few precious seconds. Max called to stop him, and I squeezed the trigger. The big animal was down within seconds, covering no more than 20 yards in his final scramble. He was just as I'd imagined he might be, a striking and mature 6×6 bull that had come in screaming and slobbering and pissing himself, and it had all culminated with a single shot at close range.

I was indeed in a good mood—and would've been hard-pressed to say that it wasn't every bit as much fun as a good turkey hunt.

Chapter Five
The Journey

My New Creed

Miles and I had been hunting together for about a decade when the 6.5 Creedmoor Craze began. Good friends have rituals, and for several enjoyable years, come nightfall in hunting camp, we would have us a little liquor, cuss, and speak ill of the Creed. We'd mostly point out that the 6.5, by God, was no .30/06. Then we'd build a fire so as to have something to poke with sticks and spit on.

But then one afternoon Miles called me and explained with rehearsed diction that he'd become a pro-staffer for the Bergara rifle company—and they wanted to send him a gun in 6.5 Creedmoor. When I asked if he intended to accept it, he became so defensive that I suspected he already had the gun in hand and possibly sighted in too.

He brought the rifle with him for our annual Tennessee whitetail hunt and used it to drop a big 8-pointer in its tracks. As we were dragging the buck out, I told Miles it was a lucky one-shot kill and had the deer run off, we'd have probably never recovered it.

That night in camp, we went toe-to-toe over his new Creed, but I eventually lost the energy to argue. He wasn't going to admit to being wrong anyway. So, we went quiet. It felt like the conclusion of a family brawl over politics, spurred by Granny's "Trump 'n' Dressin'" casserole at Thanksgiving dinner. Even without a concession, it was good to know the yelling could at least stop.

The following spring, Miles scored a new lease in Texas and invited me to come turkey hunting. Like all 6.5 Creedmoor shooters, he cannot call birds worth a damn. Still, we killed two big Rio Grande gobblers on the first morning. Later in the day, as the sun began to set and I was running out of things to say about how much better it is to call game animals close than it is to shoot them at long range, Miles suggested we go pig hunting.

"This place is covered in them," he said. "But there's a catch."

"What catch?" I asked.

"You have to shoot this." He handed me his 6.5. "This is my new favorite gun, and I'm not ashamed of saying it anymore, Brantley. If you want to shoot one of my pigs, this is what you'll use."

We sat on a mesa just before dark, watching a corn feeder positioned in a creek drainage several hundred yards below us. When I saw a large form moving through the bottom, I glassed it casually, assuming it was a steer slipping in for a bite of corn. Instead, the binos revealed a giant gray boar hog lumbering toward the feeder. I clawed for the rifle.

"Shoot that thing in the head so we don't have to go tromping through the mesquite in the dark looking for it," Miles said, staring through his own binocular.

I adjusted the scope turret a few clicks and sent a 143-grain ELD-X bullet across 300 yards of Texas. There was a *whump*, and the boar dropped in his tracks, kicked a few times, and was still. I watched it all through the scope, which, under the 6.5's minimal recoil, had barely moved.

After a while, Miles cleared his throat and said, "I'll have my rifle back now." I wasn't sure I wanted to give it back. Tomes of ballistic evidence and gun-writer acclaim can't always convince a guy the way a giant dead boar hog can. Still, I waited for a bit before I ordered my own new 6.5.

That night at camp, Miles and I poured us a little liquor and reflected on a good day.

"Have you shot one of these 6.5 PRCs?" he asked me.

"Hell no," I said. "Stupid idea."

"Totally," Miles said. "It's no .300 Win Mag, I'll tell you that."

Then we built a fire so we could have something to poke with sticks and spit on.

THE CRAIG'S LIST CAMPER

I found the 10-foot, 1970s-model camper on Craig's List soon as Michelle left for work. Over the course of the next six hours, I called and talked the owner down by a hundred bucks, and then my brother, Matt, and I drove to Tennessee to make the deal. The seller's name was Bill Kelly, and he had the camper plugged into a temporary service pole and running when we got there. "The air conditioner on this thing will freeze you out, son," he said. His house was 100 yards away, at the end of a long driveway.

I began thumbing out the 14 $100 bills and then noticed a car coming down the drive toward us. It stopped, and a bleach-blond woman named "Bae" emerged. She seized the money from Bill Kelly's hand, licked her thumb, counted the bills, stuffed them into her ample cleavage, and got back into the car without so much as a word.

I remember Bill Kelly stepping unusually close to Matt as he screamed "BAAAEEE!" at the car's taillights. Bae never checked up, but Bill settled down quickly, as if he'd long since resigned himself to this behavior. "She's never cared about anything but the money," he said. "I'll help guide you onto the hitch."

We towed the camper home and unhooked it in my driveway. I went inside to get some beer to put in its mini-fridge, and Matt grabbed two lawn chairs. We lived in town back then, with neighbors on both sides. Matt opened a beer and took a deep sip, then looked up the street one way and then down the other. Finally, he settled into his lawn chair and said, "By God, I bet you're the only one on this road who got a deal like this today."

Michelle pulled into the drive a little later, after enough time for Matt and I to have finished most of the beer. "What in the hell is this?" she asked.

"It's your new deer camp, Bae. I bought it from Bill Kelly. I figure we'll put it up out at the farm," I said.

"Bae?"

"And this," Matt said, hoisting a Keystone Light, "is a cold beer. Have you one, Mishkin."

Michelle took the beer and said, "If we're going to be seen in a piece of shit like this, I'm at least getting some pink plastic flamingos to go with it."

She and I had saved enough for a down payment on 33 acres the previous winter, a little chunk of hunting ground near the lake to call our own. The camper was the perfect complement, and it became our second home, year-round. I took the kitchen table out of it and cut up 2-by-6s to fit instead in its place, atop which we placed a full-sized mattress. There was already a couch that turned into a tiny bed on the other end of the camper, and that's where Matt slept most of catfish noodling season.

Sometimes, the deep fryer, plugged directly into the camper, would trip a breaker and cause the whole thing to lose power. But it was a quick fix and rarely interrupted our cooking long enough for the flathead to get too greasy. We cooked backstrap on the charcoal grill outside. During the summer, the proclamation about the air conditioner was true—it would freeze you out, running full bore. Come duck season, one little space heater would force you to open a window. Had you told me back then, "This is what Heaven's like," I'd have said, "I'm ready to go whenever."

But that camper's tiny walls did close in eventually. When our son, Anse, was born, my mom sat with him in the tiny camper in the evenings while Michelle and I hunted. We came in one night after dark and found Mom with tears in her eyes. She'd picked Anse up and banged his head right into the ceiling. The kid was fine, though the ceiling was dented a bit.

That June, we celebrated his first birthday at the camper with a big fish fry. In-laws skulked about in the mud with drooping paper plates of fried catfish, and Matt struggled to keep the fryer running with the air conditioner going at the same time. I knew I had a real chore ahead of me the next day, too, emptying out the 30-gallon sewage tank.

"I think we've outgrown Bill Kelly's camper," Michelle said, and I agreed. A neighbor across the road from camp had inquired about it. The tires had long since dry-rotted, and I told him that if he could just come get the thing and move it on the rims, he could have it.

"Air conditioner on this thing will freeze you out," I said as I helped guide it onto the hitch of his truck. He pulled away in a shower of sparks.

"We had fourteen hundred dollars' worth of fun in that camper, didn't we?" I asked. Michelle nodded in agreement and declared the pink flamingos would still look good no matter what type of deer camp we decided to put in its place.

The Coyote Trapper

I'd like a sticker for the back glass of my truck that says, "Proud Parent of a Kid Who Can ID the Hair in a Coyote Turd." My son, Anse, was five years old, learning to recognize sight words and count to 50. After school, I taught him how to recognize the sign left behind by wild critters and to understand why we set our traps where we did.

We learned to catch raccoons easily enough, but we both wanted a coyote. Anse asked me daily how big they are, if they stink, and if one got in a fight with a big boar raccoon, who would win? I told him that a yote would whip a boar coon but that he'd need a good day to do it. What I didn't say was that trapping coyotes had his old dad stumped. I grew up hunting and fishing for just about everything, but I wasn't a trapper. I got into it only after Anse was born, and it took a while for my skill to catch up to his enthusiasm. I'd always admired good trappers and their quiet confidence, but I was intimidated by them, too. My ineptitude at catching coyotes only drove that feeling home.

I messed with foothold traps in my shop at night and watched YouTube videos on making dirt-hole and flat sets. Good trappers say it might take a week for a coyote to find a set, and we checked ours every 24 hours. We had traps in the ground most of the winter, and our failure rate stood at 100 percent. Yet, Anse sprung out of bed day after day, pulled on his tiny coveralls, and went with me to check traps by light of a headlamp almost every morning before school. We found traps that had been ignored, traps washed out by rain, and traps dug up by coyotes that weren't fooled.

Then one Friday afternoon, with just an hour of daylight left, Anse and I took a walk and cut a set of fresh coyote prints in a two-track dirt road. We bedded three Duke traps in a 100-yard stretch. That night, Anse told me, "I know we're going to catch one."

It was a Saturday, and so I persuaded him to wait until after daylight to check the line by saying the coyotes might move best right before sunrise. He paced in his coveralls with a box of apple juice, looking out the window. Finally, he said, "Daddy, I can see. Let's go."

A hundred yards from the very first set, I could see pointed ears darting back and forth. I finally got to say the line I'd been rehearsing in my head all winter. "Buddy, we've got a coyote!" It was a rare cold and clear day, a break from the usual February rain and mud. Anse told me his breath looked like smoke. Then, matter-of-factly, he added, "Coyotes move best when it's cold and sunny."

He's got a quiet confidence about him that I admire.

A Limit with Wade

Some say a big shellcracker is the most mysterious fish in freshwater. Properly called a redear sunfish, they're three times the size of a keeper bluegill, on average, but just as delicious. But they're notoriously finicky, apt to ignore a nightcrawler threaded onto an Aberdeen hook but then inhale a redworm, thrown to the same spot on the same rig the very next cast. Most of the time they hug the bottom, where they probe gravel bars for snails. When you haven't caught one in a year, their power against light spinning tackle is startling.

For a few short days late in the spring, when the weather is warm and the moon is just so, and if you've been a good person most of the year and hold your mouth just right, you might find shellcrackers on the bed and catch a mess of them. One time, and only one time, I caught my daily limit of 20 shellcrackers from a single bed. Wade Bourne caught his limit, too. He was standing at the stern of my 16-foot johnboat, threading redworms onto his hook and smiling and laughing as if he hadn't spent an entire, storied career doing things just like that.

Wade didn't know it—or maybe he did—but he was a mentor and a hero to me. From the time I was about 12 years old, I knew I wanted to be an outdoor writer when I grew up. But I never cared about going to Africa to hunt dangerous game, nor did I grow up reading Capstick, Ruark, or O'Conner. Instead, I devoured the hunting and fishing articles of the 1990s, of which there were a bunch. I kept stacks of magazines like *Game & Fish*, *Bassmaster*, *Southern Outdoors*, *Buckmasters*, *Fur-Fish-Game*, *Outdoor Life*, and *Field & Stream* in my room. I'd look for names like Zumbo, Hanback, and Winke, but Wade Bourne was my favorite. You could find his stories in most of those magazines, but he was also a television and radio host with a kind, clear Southern voice that was instantly recognizable.

Wade hunted and fished the same places that I did and for the same critters. On television he shot gadwalls and squirrels and rabbits and whitetails. I remember one show when he hunted hogs with a Smith & Wesson revolver. I'd never seen anyone hunt with a handgun, and for many years following that, I was a teenager obsessed with it. Thirty years before #GetBit was a thing on Instagram, Wade was filming catfish noodling in Mississippi. And long before I met him in person, I had a copy of *Southern Outdoors* with

Wade on the cover, standing knee deep in a Tennessee creek with a spinning rod in one hand and a nice smallmouth in the other.

That guy has it figured out, I thought.

Wade lived less than two hours from me my entire life, but I never knew it. Nor did I realize he was a graduate of Murray State University, where I went to school, too. It took living in New York City for a summer to finally meet him in person. I was 19 years old and an intern at *Outdoor Life*. I worked in a cubicle next to the editor's office, where I spent my days checking the accuracy of websites and phone numbers that were about to be printed. One of the editors had told me the horror story of the intern who didn't verify a phone number, and an adult talk hotline had made it into print.

I lived in Greenwich Village and walked 30 blocks to work on Park Avenue each day, wearing nice khakis and button-up shirts that my mom bought me, especially for that summer. I'd come from a tiny town in Kentucky, and every day I wondered how living in that loud and bustling concrete hell would lead to a job where I got to fish creeks for smallmouths and shoot pigs with .44 magnum revolvers.

And then one day, Wade Bourne walked in and stood next to my cubicle to talk to the editor. He was dressed in nice clothes, too, and the editor introduced me as the summer intern. When Wade heard me talk, he smiled and gave me his undivided attention. "You sound like you're from closer to where I live than up here," he said. "You're learning to get into this business?"

I wanted to gush—to tell him that I'd seen him on TV when I was 10 years old, wrestling catfish in the Yazoo River, to tell him that I'd read that story he'd written about calling up a gobbler for his young son, Hampton, who missed the gobbler with a little double-barreled 20-gauge, and that that story had made me feel better once upon a time because, like Hampton, I missed the first turkey I ever shot at, too, when I was little and also hunting with my dad. I wanted to talk about squirrel hunting and bream fishing and all the things that Wade seemed to enjoy just as much as I did. I wanted to say that my life's ambition was to be just like him.

But mercifully I didn't say much more than, "Yes, sir, I love to hunt, fish, and tell stories."

But Wade must've heard something extra. My dad owned a one-man-show law office in Dawson Springs, Kentucky, and the next week, he called me in New York. "You're not going to believe this!" he said. "Wade Bourne, the guy on TV, called my office to tell me that he'd met you and that he just wanted to say he was impressed."

Two years later I was 21 and standing neck deep in the muddy water of the Yazoo River. A hard-boiled Mississippian named Bob stood next to me, glaring, calling me "Wade Junior," and telling me to jump into the water and catch a catfish with my hands. I remember being worried about losing my wedding band since I'd been married only three weeks, and it still felt out of place on my hand.

Wade had shared the contact information for his Mississippi catfish noodlers, with the warning that they were rough around the edges, and they were. But I ran my bare hand into a cypress box the size of a coffin and grabbed the flathead waiting inside by the lower jaw. He rolled and thrashed, peeling enough skin from my knuckles as to leave faint scars that I wear to this day, but I slung him over the gunwale of the nearest johnboat. I came home, wrote a story about it, and sold it to *Field & Stream*—my first. Wade told me that people were always mesmerized by stories and videos about people grabbing catfish and probably always would be. I don't know how many noodling stories and videos I've done in the near 20 years since, but it's been several.

Wade put my name in for an associate editor's job at DU a few years later. He was the voice and face of that organization: the host of their television show and the field editor of their magazine. He was gray by then with bad knees, at an age of which many would retire, but why would you retire if you were Wade Bourne and loved it all as much as he did?

I worried that when I left DU after just two years to try my hand at freelancing full-time, I would seem ungrateful for the opportunity, and perhaps Wade would be upset. But he simply wished me luck and asked that I call him if the shellcracker bite got good. One day in late May, when the weather seemed right and the full moon was just past, I called Wade and invited him to come fishing with me. He was there at daybreak the next day.

We caught a few bluegills right off the bat that morning, but the shellcrackers were being themselves. I had a milk run of spots I liked to check, but they were mostly empty. Late in the morning with only a few stops left on the list, I was afraid we might end the day skunked. But then I stopped my boat 20 yards off a rocky point, where I'd caught a redear or two in the past, and fired a long cast with a redworm on a drop-shot rig. When I took up slack, my line was already swinging toward deep water. A little tension bent the ultralight rod into a neat bow, and the reel's drag buzzed. A giant shellcracker rolled alongside the boat, the size of which where, for a second, you worry about the strength of 4-pound test. But Wade scooped it up in my net, a quivering bream so thick that it was more practical to lip than grasp in the middle. "What a beautiful fish!" Wade said, a line that could've been scripted for TV or a radio show but was shared only with me and purely of genuine appreciation for being there.

"We better drop the anchor here for a minute," I said. The spot was easy to see, as the redears had worked up a cloud of silt next to the shoreline, just at the end of a long cast. We didn't dare get any closer. I stuck with a drop shot, but Wade rigged his redworms under a tiny split-shot sinker and a pencil float just because, he said, he loved to watch a cork disappear. He got to see plenty of that. We caught shellcrackers almost every cast, and in little more than an hour our limits were filled.

Wade and I stayed in regular touch and often talked about those redears. In the summer of 2016, the same year he received the Homer Circle Fishing Communicator Award, he called me for advice on booking an elk hunt. He'd had surgery on his knees and was getting around better than ever. Since I was the hunting editor of *Field & Stream* and traveling the world to hunt big game, he thought I might know of a place to go. I mentioned that he should call my buddy, Miles. We talked for a while before bad reception dropped the call. I texted Wade and told him we'd follow up on that elk hunt later, and he texted back and said it was good catching up. He died that December, at age 69, of a heart attack while cutting a Christmas tree.

I still fish that point, and though no shellcracker spot is a guarantee, it's as reliable as any I know if you catch it on just the right late-spring day. Sometimes, when I do catch one, I'll smile and say out loud, to no one in particular, "What a beautiful fish." I genuinely appreciate being there. And all these years later, I still wouldn't mind being a little more like Wade.

Confessions of a Turkey Purist

It's easy to become a purist turkey hunter when you stumble into a mob of two-year-old gobblers on opening morning. I was sneaking along the spine of a hardwood ridge, working toward a distant bird that I'd heard earlier, when the mob sounded off suddenly, less than 100 yards ahead. Their gobbles were jarring and terrible, like children who'd been given box calls, loosely bound with rubber bands, and told to make a ruckus.

That sounds so awful, it has to be a gang of jakes, I thought to myself. All alone, I then wondered, *Could I get a jake back to the truck without another hunter seeing me?*

Gaaarrrobbble! The birds roared again, and I decided to call them up into shotgun range for a good, close look before I entirely wrote off any jake shooting. I sat against a broad white oak and yelped three times. The turkeys answered immediately, so close that I could feel concussion at the end of the gobbles. Seconds later, to my right, I heard drumming and footfalls in the leaves. I shifted my hips and gun in that direction, pressed my cheek on the stock, and clicked off the safety.

Instead of jakes, three longbeards strutted into the sunshine 25 yards away, their white heads matching the blooming dogwoods. I didn't care which of the turkeys I shot; the second bird in line separated himself from the other two first, and so I took him. He had a 10-inch beard and had been fooled fair and square on public land, in the timber, without a decoy or fan.

I never want to kill a turkey any other way, I thought, feeling like the purest of purists in that moment. But it was easy to forget that there were weeks of turkey season still ahead of me.

Old-school turkey hunting is having a moment right now, and it's rooted in the best of intentions. Many modern turkey purists are much like me; they're in their forties, from the Southeast or Midwest, and they learned to turkey hunt in the late 1990s and early 2000s. That was the height of the restoration and when turkey populations were at all-time highs. Advances in gear and tactics were happening fast. Better calls, hyperrealistic decoys, pop-up ground blinds, 60-yard shotguns, and tactics like fanning and reaping all came about within a decade, and they all made it incrementally easier to kill turkeys.

In those days, it seemed we'd never run out of turkeys to kill, either. But then we got a taste of reality. I remember the first five-day stretch I went without seeing or hearing a gobbler, the longest dry spell I'd ever had in a spring. Unfortunately, it wasn't a fluke; within a few short springs, sitting down to a gobbling turkey on an April morning seemed to become the exception rather than the rule. Hunters across the Eastern United States took notice, and what followed was a groundswell of hunter concern over the country's dwindling wild turkey resource.

As a result, over the past six years, there's been an unprecedented amount of new research dedicated to wild turkeys, and leading biologists have been able to share their research results in real time through social media, podcasts, and articles. Because of all this, modern turkey hunters undoubtedly know more about the wild turkey life cycle than ever before (it wouldn't be unusual to hear the words "exploded lek" in a Mississippi coffee shop in March, for example).

We've learned that turkey population declines can be linked to a variety of factors, including predation, bad weather, habitat loss, farming practices—and hunting pressure. Research has suggested that if dominant gobblers in particular are removed from the flock too early in the spring, it can disrupt the whole breeding cycle. As a result, a number of states have moved their opening days later, reduced bag limits, and, in a few cases, banned tactics that are especially effective on dominant, early season gobblers, like decoys, fanning, and reaping. It's too early to say for certain that any of it is working, but some states have reported better hatches recently. Last spring, a number of Southern states even reported their best harvests—despite lowered bag limits—in years, too.

This all has many avid turkey hunters embracing classic tactics, even to the extreme in some cases. Although few regulations have actually been passed to outlaw particular equipment or tactics, the new purist's code nonetheless calls for voluntary prohibitions on fanning, decoys, ground blinds, ditch slipping, hunting on private land, ambushing turkeys on chufa plots, Tungsten Super Shot, and jake shooting. Mess up, and maybe you won't get a ticket from the game warden, but game wardens didn't give the Salem witches tickets for their shenanigans, either.

This new purist culture is probably helping turkey populations in the big picture, and I do my best to be a part of it. Most of the time, it's not hard. Traveling light in the timber with no decoys is how I learned to hunt, and it's always been my favorite way to kill a turkey.

But sometimes I also remember how much fun I used to have when, if a turkey wouldn't come to me, I'd just go to him, crawling through the cow shit with a fan held over my head, like a heathen. I think maybe if I can stick to being a purist most of the time, like 60 percent, it's good enough. I also think nobody cares if a fly fisherman digs up the occasional redworm.

If I acted like a purist in the early season in Tennessee last year, I slipped when I got to Nebraska. For the past decade or more, I've wrapped my season out there, on the edge of the Sandhills in mid-May. I can usually scratch out a gobbler or two in that open country, but rarely without taking an ass kicking first. Miles of walking, glassing, and maneuvering are frequently required to get on gobblers out there. Some of those turkeys will come to a call, but most of them are taken by using the terrain to creep and crawl into shotgun range—sometimes with the help of a dried turkey fan.

I'd experienced the ass-kicking part of the trip for two straight days. On the third evening, my buddy Tim—who'd tagged out early—roosted a flock of turkeys in a big cottonwood creek drainage overlooking an alfalfa field, not far from camp. "There were three strutters in the bunch," he said. "I bet they pitch right into that alfalfa in the morning."

I set up 70 yards from them in the dark, but instead of pitching into the alfalfa in front of me, the entire flock set their wings and sailed into the field on the other side of the creek drainage, 500 yards away. I could see three good longbeards strutting with hens, and I watched as they fed into the Sandhills. I knew the country where they were going, and so I stood up and started jogging to get ahead of them. I brought a dried jake fan with me, too, just in case.

A half hour later, I was slipping up a ditch, through the cedars and yucca plants, and I knew I had to be close to the turkeys. Suddenly, they gobbled from up on the hillside, directly above me. I slithered up a cow path on the creek bank, peaked over the brim of the hill, and spotted hens bugging just 30 yards away. The three gobblers were strutting another 30 yards behind them. I slowly raised the jake fan into sight, twisted it slightly right and left, and made three soft yelps. The gobblers roared back and began marching my way.

I didn't care which of them I shot, but the second one in line separated from the others first, and I took him at maybe 25 yards. He was a nice two-year-old bird with a thick beard and the buff fan tips of a Merriam's hybrid. Truth be told, I worked harder to kill that turkey than any of the others I'd taken last spring.

Not that it matters now, of course, because it's a new season—and I'm a purist again, waiting to stumble into a mob of two-year-olds and leaving that jake fan in the truck.

Dad's Call

There's an old split-rail fence at Mom and Dad's place along the edge of the horse pasture. The creek is down below the pasture, and in the spring, there's a gobbler roosted somewhere along its banks often as not. Late in the evening, if I lean against the fence and owl hoot, he'll gobble if he's there. That night, he was there.

I expected as much because Dad had seen the turkey strutting in the pasture just the day before and had set up on him. The bird had gobbled but not come in. I was glad to hear Dad had given him a try, though, because the fire he once had for turkey hunting—and hunting everything, really—has faded. There was nothing I would've liked more than to see him shoot that turkey.

I walked into the cabin with the good news. Dad was watching CNN at two clicks shy of maximum volume, the television set buzzing like a cheap sound system. But he turned it down and asked, "Hear him?"

"Hell yeah. Roosted right over the creek. We're going to have to get there and set up *early*." I emphasized the last word, and Dad's eyes narrowed the way they always do when I hint at taking the lead on, well, anything.

"How early?"

I saw my first gobbler called into gun range 30 years ago. I was sitting between Dad's knees, cradling a 20-gauge as the turkey gobbled over and again, first on the limb, then on the ground. Dad whispered to me, "I'll tap your neck when he's close enough."

He used slate and box calls, but Dad was talented enough with his natural voice to win a few local calling contests. He yelped softly, and the bird popped into view just 30 yards away. The tap on my neck, the roar of the shotgun, and the gobbler winging out of sight could've been one fluid moment. I fought back tears but couldn't hold them all. Dad smiled and said, "Do you want to quit?"

"No."

"Good."

That single morning shaped my whole life, to this very moment. How do you repay something like that?

I knew we needed to get up at 3:45, but I also knew that if I suggested that, I'd have to argue why, and I wasn't up for it. As he's gotten older, Dad likes to sleep in, sometimes for a long time. "Four thirty, but we've got to go when we get up," I told him.

At 4:50, I was pacing the cabin while Dad fussed with contact lenses and nursed a cup of black coffee. I stepped onto the porch and strained my eyes at the sky, as if staring at them would keep the stars out just a bit longer. When I went back in, Dad was wearing camo pants but fishing around in the hunting closet. "Have you got some extra shells?" he asked.

"Yep, I have you covered there," I said. "TSS number nines."

"*Nines?*" he said. "I like fours."

"Dad, these are . . ." I stopped myself. "I have some lead fours, too, that will be fine."

He walked back over to his coffee, and I stepped back out onto the porch, where I heard the first notes of the dawn chorus and could see well out into the pasture. "Dad, we have to get going!" I hissed, slinging a bag of decoys over my shoulder.

"Okay!" he huffed and splashed his coffee into the sink.

We crossed the fence, and I could see the young leaves on the maples on the edge of the creek at the end of the pasture, where we talked about setting up. It was legal shooting light by the time we sat down. Two distant birds sounded off, but near us, it was silent.

"You think we scared him?" Dad whispered.

"Yes, 100 percent, we scared him. He watched us walk across that pasture and set those decoys, plain as day."

"I don't think so."

I shrugged. The gobbles from the birds in the distance were faint but steady. Suddenly I saw Dad twist to his right and shoulder his 870. My heart jumped, as I was thinking the roosted tom had walked in silently and Dad had spotted him. Instead, I saw the wake of a beaver swimming down the creek. I knew what was coming. Dad hates beavers with a real passion because he's fought their efforts to flood our bottoms for most of his life. He hit the beaver in the head with the entirety of a $10 TSS shotgun shell, which I'd handed to him in the dark, telling him it was a good No. 4 lead load. Geese flushed off the creek, and the horses stampeded from the pasture as the blast reverberated through the timber. Dad racked the slide and regarded the smoking hull with a smile.

"Killed that fucker dead," he said. "You think we ought to move?"

We snuck our way toward the other end of the farm, where the distant birds had since gone silent, eventually setting up in the shagbarks just above the old cabin, where I killed my first squirrel years and years ago. I stuck the decoys 20 yards ahead on the right, to Dad's side. I cut hard on a mouth call, and any expectations of relaxing in the sunshine vanished when a gobbler with marbles in his throat fired off 100 yards away. Dad immediately pulled his shotgun to his knee.

I called again, and the bird cut me off with another deep gobble. He was coming fast. For five minutes it was back and forth, *call—gobble*, and I knew we were about to see him. I was watching the rise just beyond the decoys, expecting the tom to materialize at any second. But then, nothing. I yelped, but no response. No drumming, no walking in the leaves. Fifteen minutes passed, and somehow, I thought, that turkey had busted us, too.

Then Dad yelped with his voice. It sounded old. Scratchy. Out of practice. "Damn, we sound desperate," I thought to myself—but the turkey roared back, right on top of us. I broke into a grin and then heard drumming. I looked all around the decoys, but the turkey wasn't there. Cocking my eyes to the left—my side—I could see the gobbler standing in full strut and plain view, about 30 yards away. Dad couldn't shoot without putting the muzzle of his gun next to my face.

"Kill him," he said. I didn't move. "Will, shoot him! He's going to get away if you don't!"

The bird spun his fan to me and drummed, and I snapped my gun to my shoulder. Dad yelped again, and the turkey dropped into a ruffle, craning his neck. He flopped down the hill at the shot and came to a rest just feet from our decoys. I stood and shook my head in disgust.

"What's a matter with you?" Dad asked.

"I really wanted you to shoot that bird," I said.

"Hell, I've been calling them in for you to shoot for 25 years," he said. "I don't know why that should change now. Let's go eat breakfast."

Mom took our picture with the turkey, next to the split-rail fence. It wasn't the exact hunt I'd envisioned. But I think in Dad's mind, it played out perfectly.

Little Lockjaw

Anse had just turned eight—old enough, in my book, if not Michelle's, to fish the pond by himself. Although it's only 200 yards from the front door, Michelle gave Anse a two-way radio and cell phone and strict instructions to check in every 10 minutes and to be home in 30. I told him to keep some 12-inch bass for dinner if he caught them. But I knew his designs were on taxidermy for his room. I'd told him many times that a largemouth had to be 5 pounds before I'd pay to have it stuffed.

Anse put his Case pen knife into a hip pocket, and he carried a bucket with a package of his favorite swimbaits, a stringer, and a Capris Sun. He hugged Michelle around the neck, nodded at me, and walked toward the pond, spinning rod in hand, without looking back once.

She and I sat on the porch, staring at the radio, and within five minutes we heard static and a small voice. "Deeds, it's Anse. I'm at the pond. Over."

"Okay, buddy, good luck," I told him.

It was a good day for a boy to fish. The radio soon crackled again: "Deeds! I caught a 3-pounder, but I'm going to let him go! I have two keepers in the bucket already! Over!" My phone then buzzed with a blurry picture of an 18-inch, potbellied bass laying alongside his rod in the green grass. "This is the best day of my life! Over!"

I strutted a bit as I plugged in my electric knife and gathered a cutting board and plastic bowl for fillets. "I told you he'd be fine," I said to Michelle. His time at the pond was running out, but she'd already agreed to 10 extra minutes if he radioed and asked for it.

But then we heard the hysterical, unmistakable cries of our child in distress. We saw him coming, shuffling across the field toward us, lugging the bucket, and with his fishing rod held in the air like a torch. We ran toward him, screaming his name and envisioning the worst; twin holes in his leg from the fangs of a cottonmouth, perhaps, or a pocketknife wound, down to the bone in his hand.

Instead, I found the spool of his spinning reel stripped clean, 6-pound monofilament entangled in blackberry briars for a full trail length behind him. Anse's face was red and swollen, with tracks from tears onto his neck. I caught my breath as I put my hands on his shoulders and checked him for obvious injury. "Buddy, what's wrong?"

"I had him," he said. "Deeds, I had the 5-pounder. I hooked him on my swimbait and pulled him up on the muddy spot next to the feeder, and I was trying to take a picture of him, and he flopped, and I tried to grab him, but my line broke, and he got back in the water, and he took my bait with him!"

I knelt in the field, with him crying into my shoulder. Two little bass sloshed in the bucket; he'd packed them across the field in a full gallon of water. I asked Anse for his stringer so they'd be easier to carry, and later, before we cleaned them, I even convinced him to hold them up for a picture.

Every boy needs a story of a big fish. Although I had to hide it, I couldn't help but smile, knowing that Anse's story was just beginning.

Larry's Legacy

The red Chevy S-10 was tiny, the way 1980s-era four-banger pickups were, and perhaps that made the buck in the bed of it seem larger than life. But the deer would've been big on a flatbed trailer, too. It was a massive, mainframe 8-pointer with beams that curled like flames from a hardwood campfire and forked G-2s so long they could've been used to stake bean plants.

The buck even looked large next to Larry, who didn't step out of the S-10 so much as unfold from it. He was 6-foot-4, give or take, and wrapped in lean muscle built from a lifetime of working cattle, hauling hay, and wrestling implements. He worked the farm in the evenings, his second job, after he'd put in his eight hours at the plant.

Larry banked his vacation, using some of it for turkey hunting in April but most of it in November, for rifle season. He hunted the same farm that he'd worked since he was 14, where he'd learned to be a deer hunter. The first time I walked into his house, I saw shoulder mounts of two whitetails that were bigger than any I'd ever seen on the hoof. Book deer, or close to it.

"What did those things score?" I asked, but he shrugged and smiled and said, "I've never been too worried about that." He'd tell me the stories of getting them without missing a detail, though. He shot the biggest one on a foggy morning, on the bank of the pond dam, through a blackberry thicket with a .30/06 that he called Old Stomper.

We liked telling hunting stories, Larry and me. It was an unlikely friendship since I was the skinny, 17-year-old boy who was dating Michelle, his youngest daughter. She and I had been to the movies the afternoon that he killed the giant 8-pointer, and we'd rushed back to meet him at dark to see how his hunt had gone. This was before cell phones.

The three of us stood around the tailgate of that little S-10, looking at that buck, clouds of breath blowing in the nighttime November chill as Larry told of how the deer had stepped out of the creek bottom, near the canebrake, 10 minutes before dark. He smiled, laughed, shouldered an imaginary rifle. It's been more than a quarter century since, but sometimes I think, if I'm quiet enough, I can still hear him telling that story.

Larry was good at hunting trophy deer. The last one he had shoulder-mounted was in 2017, a typical 10-pointer that I guess would score about 150. He didn't measure it, of course, but he did pose for a picture with it, alongside Michelle and Anse, who was three at the time.

So much of how Larry hunted was at odds with today's mainstream advice. His time in the woods was restricted to the weekends and vacation days he could get from work. He couldn't afford to stay at home to keep from over-pressuring his spots. He didn't worry much about the wind, and he never looked at a hunting app in his life. He simply got in his stand before daylight and got out after dark, with a short break for lunch.

That's not to say he was always passive. He'd seen the giant 8-pointer the evening before he killed it from across the river bottoms, 500 yards away or farther. So, the next day he snuck closer and set up on the edge of the creek, next to a canebrake in a folding dove chair. That night, when the buck came back out, it was just 90 yards away.

Larry's gear was minimalistic but purposeful. His go-to rifle was a Model 700 in .270, with a 3-9×40 scope, but one year he surprised us all when he sprung for a brand-new Ruger .300 Win Mag, Leupold scope, and laser rangefinder. He had designs on being able to kill a buck from across the bottoms, at 500 yards if he needed to, but he switched back to his .270 the following year. He embraced trail cameras and ran them all summer and fall. He'd check his cards once a week, download photos on the home computer, and then tell Mary, his wife and Michelle's mom, to e-mail them to us. After that, he'd call to be sure Michelle had gotten them.

He must've had a thousand pictures of that last big 10-pointer that he shot, from his box blind, with his .270.

Anse shot his first deer, a 140-class 10-pointer, when he was six years old. Michelle and I had hoped that a doe or spike would be the kid's first deer, but that's not what stepped out. I was worried my son would be spoiled on deer hunting, but Larry wasn't. "I told you that boy would get a good one," he said. "He'll be hooked for life."

It was August 2022, and Larry and Anse had been working on stands and checking trail cameras. Anse was eight years old, ahead of his third deer season. Although he'd killed several whitetails, he hadn't yet shot a buck from Papaw's stand. Larry wanted to change that.

But Anse came home and said Papaw's back had been hurting him. Larry thought for a while that he'd twisted a muscle. But the pain persisted and got worse, and just after Halloween, he was diagnosed with cancer. It was serious, the doctors said. They'd need to run more tests to know how serious and what the treatment options were.

Larry had no plans of being given a timeline or treatment. He went home to live as long as he could, maybe for another deer season. And he planned to sit with Anse and me on the afternoon of opening day, November 12. We'd stocked the box blind with an extra heater and propane, and we thought perhaps we could drive the truck to the back door of the blind, where Larry could step in and not have to walk much.

Two days earlier, when we'd made the plan, it could've worked. The forecast for opening afternoon was perfect, with a rare dusting of snow on the ground. But Larry could scarcely stand from his favorite chair. He called Anse to his chairside, wrapped a frail arm around him, and said, "You go hunt my stand and keep watch. There are some nice 8-pointers over there and an old big one, too."

The sit was magic. We'd no more than closed the box blind door when a spike came crashing through the timber, wild-eyed after a pair of does. The noise settled, and an hour later I saw more does coming, with a nice 8-pointer in tow. Larry's blind overlooked a dozer lane in the trees, and the does crossed it, 60 yards in front of us.

"Get ready, buddy, he's going to be right behind them," I whispered. But the rifle was already out the window, and I'd heard the safety click and knew the kid was steady. The buck materialized, quartering sharply to us, and I didn't have to explain to Anse to hold on the front of the shoulder, at the crease of the neck. The buck scrambled across the dozer lane at the shot, and we found heavy blood in the snow. The deer was dead next to the creek, the one that flows through the bottoms and eventually trickles out near the canebrake.

Larry stood from his chair that night, one of the last times he was able, and walked out onto the porch. And there the four of us stood, him and Anse, Michelle and me, as Anse laughed and smiled and told the story of his buck, even using his hands to shoulder an imaginary rifle, our clouds of breath blowing in the nighttime November chill.

Lost and Found

There was no logical reason not to go elk hunting, but it was still unsettling to ride into the same mountains where a man had just gone missing. He was a hunter himself, 79 years old, and he'd gone scouting five days earlier. He'd radioed at one point to tell his wife that he was 20 minutes out and then was never heard from again.

Ryan and I had been planning our trip for months. We'd drawn muzzleloader tags and booked a September drop camp with Travis Reed, a couple drainages over from where I'd killed my first elk a few years earlier. When we arrived at the trailhead, the search-and-rescue mission was active, and Missing Person signs were tacked to trees. Travis said to send an InReach message if we saw anything.

A wildfire had ravaged the area we were hunting a few years earlier, making it even easier to disappear. Deadfalls of charred pine crisscrossed the trails, and they were concealed under a thatch of saplings that had bloomed following the fire. Our canvas tent was at about 9,000 feet, in a quarter-acre clearing surrounded by miserable jungle. Travis dropped us off, wished us luck, and turned and disappeared into the growth with the horses.

Ryan and I each had GPS units, offline maps downloaded, and paper maps, too. But in that tangle, it felt as if even stepping out to pee carried the risk of getting lost. Regardless, season opened the next morning, and we were there to hunt. At sunset we hiked to a peak behind camp, sipped a flask, and listened for bugles. The mountains were silent.

We decided to start in the drainage behind camp the next morning. There was dark timber at the bottom, and Travis had mentioned a spring where they'd been on elk before. We worked our way down slowly, stopping occasionally to call and noting elk sign, but nothing fresh. We eventually rested in a small meadow to cook some freeze-dried Chili Mac, and that's when the silence broke. The sounds of an approaching helicopter grew from a distant hum to an overhead roar.

The red chopper flew over us treetop high, made a loop, and then came back, obviously flying a search grid. Ryan and I hiked back up the mountainside to camp, where we spotted movement on the opposite ridge. A search crew with dogs was picking their way through the brush and glassing back at us. "Seems like they think that fellow could be somewhere here close to us," Ryan said. In that stuff, he could've been 50 yards from the tent without us ever knowing.

We struck out in the opposite direction that evening, and it seemed to be a mistake at first, as the first half mile was a punishing crawl over and through a snarl of deadfalls. But clearing those, we stepped onto an elk trail and followed it into a stand of aspens where, almost immediately, we found fresh rubs and tracks. We sat to glass and listen, and as the shadows darkened, I watched two elk walk across a burned hillside a thousand yards away. They were out of sight by the time I could say "elk," but both looked to be bulls, and they were headed in our general direction. We sprang to our feet and rushed ahead.

We crested the next ridge and overlooked a green, open draw. Suspecting the elk were in the bottom of it, Ryan and I leaned against two aspens, maybe 10 yards apart, and I made a soft, whiny bugle. From across the draw, we were answered by a deep glunk. I cow called, and the bull responded with a full but distant bugle. He seemed forever away, with no more than 20 minutes of daylight left. "This would be a good spot to be sitting in the morning," I whispered to Ryan. "I don't think he's going to get here before dark, though. Maybe we should ease out."

But we stood still as the deadfalls. I pulled the cow call up and mewed again, and the responding bugle was guttural and deafening.

I sloughed my pack onto the ground and rested the fore-end of the muzzleloader against the aspen in front of me.

"Here he comes," Ryan said, lowering his binoculars. "Right there, 60 yards, legal bull."

"Shoot him," I whispered, but Ryan couldn't shoulder his gun without the bull seeing him. I cocked the hammer on my gun, and when the bull clopped into my shooting lane, I aligned the open sights on the crease of his shoulder and fired. In the low light, the blast and smoke obscured everything, but Ryan immediately said, "You hit him hard!" I'd put two speed loaders in my pocket, and I scrambled to fish one of them out and pour loose powder with shaking hands.

"Let's shoot him again if we can," I said, and we both stepped ahead, leaving our packs at the trees behind us. The bull was bedded just over the hillside, 50 yards away, looking down the draw.

"Back me up," I said, but Ryan's gun was already shouldered. I shot the bull again in his bed, and he staggered to his feet. Ryan fired, too, and the elk turned and disappeared into the draw behind a settling cloud of white smoke. I knew the elk was mortally hit, likely three times, but also that elk are incredibly tough and easy to lose in country like that. I fished the last speed loader from my pocket and topped off the rifle.

"Here," Ryan hissed and tossed me his last speed loader. "I'm going back for the packs before we lose them."

I scrambled down the hillside and spotted the bull's rack, still upright, another 70 yards ahead. He'd bedded again but was alive. I caught my breath and crept to within 30 yards before the bull stood. I did my best to hold on his heart and fired again. Once again, the bull crashed down the mountainside, but this time it stopped and staggered. I was emptying the last shot into my gun when he finally fell for good, with four .50-caliber holes behind his shoulder. Ryan came jogging down the hill.

"I was grabbing the packs, and then I heard that last shot, so I just grabbed bullets and dropped a pin," he said. "Is he down?" I smiled and pointed ahead.

We took two quick photos, and then it was dark, in woods that can swallow you in the light. I had a flashlight and pocketknife on me, and so I started gutting the bull while Ryan hiked back up to get our packs. Soon enough, I rolled the guts down the hill and propped the quarters open with a limb to cool.

I sat next to the bull in the dark and the silence, comforted somewhat by the .45 on my hip but also knowing that without my pack, I had no water, no way of starting a fire, and no GPS. I couldn't see Ryan's headlamp, either. Losing your pack and then your buddy is just the type of thing that ends up killing you in country like that.

I stood and paced, watching for the flash of a headlamp. Nothing. Ten minutes passed. Then twenty. Could I find my way back to the packs without a pin? Was Ryan turned around now, looking for me?

"Ryan?" I called out, shining my flashlight. "Ryan?"

Nothing. I forced myself to stand still, wait, and be confident that he wasn't lost, just taking a while. Then in the dark, up above, a limb broke, and I saw a flash of light.

"Hey," Ryan yelled.

I breathed a sigh of relief and rushed up the hillside to help him. In the mountains, it's not just the weather than can turn on a dime. One simple mistake can quickly turn into a tragedy. We learned later that the fellow hunter who'd gone missing in the same area had had a lifetime of experience—and he's still never been found.

"I want you to know, carrying both those packs at once is a chore," Ryan said, spinning the top off his water bottle.

"Yeah. Wait till we start packing this elk out," I said.

That night, over a jet-boil stove, we fried fresh elk tenderloin for dinner, thankful that we'd gone hunting—and settling in and getting comfortable as much as the mountains would let us.

20 Summers of Blood Sport

I wrestled my first flathead catfish in the summer of 2005, under the guidance of a Mississippian named Bob, a man who would be under investigation for murder the following year. But that day, on the Yazoo River, I reached into a coffin-shaped box, barehanded, and grabbed the catfish that was inside by its lower jaw. Its head shook and thrashed across my knuckles and fingers and palms, and I could feel the skin shearing away as it did. But I held on and threw the fish into the nearest boat, and there were Mississippians in boats all around, drunk on the violence—and some beer, too—like Romans in the Colosseum.

That flathead's bite had gone more than skin deep, figuratively speaking anyway. All that following winter, I talked about grabbing catfish. My buddies and I would be sitting in layout blinds on mudflats, waiting for gadwalls, and I'd point out a hole in a cypress stump and declare that it'd be a good spot for a cat.

I drove them nuts, Michelle, too, but there were flatheads in the rivers and lakes around home, and I wanted to learn to grab them. Michelle's mom, Mary, who's a world-class junk peddler, had a collection of plastic 55-gallon barrels in storage that she'd been saving for something special. She cut flathead-sized holes into them and gifted them to me. On a February day in a sideways snow, my buddy Tim and I pulled on waders, took the barrels, and anchored them to the riverbank. I worked with a purpose, and Tim helped, but only because it was February and he had nothing better to do. When the water got high enough, I reasoned, catfish would get into them to spawn, and they'd be good spots to go noodling.

The barrels all washed away except for one, and that following June I wrestled a 16-pound flathead out of it, barehanded again, and slung it over the gunwale of my johnboat, where it flopped and thrashed at Michelle's feet. Tim was in his boat, watching the whole thing. None of us had ever caught a flathead that big on a rod and reel; it was a fish that when fried up, belly and cheek meat included, fed six people.

A few days later, we caught a flathead that bottomed out a 50-pound scale.

When I was a kid, noodling was an underground style of fishing practiced only on the fringes. First time I saw it, I was watching weekend outdoor television—there was no Outdoor Channel then—and Wade Bourne's show *Southern Outdoors* had a spot about handfishing in Mississippi. I didn't know it at the time, but I'd get to know Wade a few years later, and he put me in touch with those same guys he fished with for my story. Bob was their ringleader.

By then, noodling was better known—and even becoming a part of pop culture, thanks to the 2001 release of *Okie Noodling*, an hour-long documentary that profiled legendary handfishermen like Lee McFarland against the backdrop of the Okie Noodling catfish tournament—an event that still goes on today. Okie Noodling is more than 20 years old now but as captivating to watch today as it was then.

We spent Junes and Julys through the late 2000s probing for holes along rocky shorelines with our feet and daring one another to reach in first to see if something was inside and willing to bite an intrepid hand. We'd party at night after noodling all day, soaking catfish wounds with peroxide and whiskey and listening to Pantera.

Michelle once said, "Who needs tattoos when you got real scars?"

I took a job in Memphis, and Michelle and I lived there two years, long enough to know we're not city people. One afternoon I could stand it no more, and so I quit my job, and on a whim and unemployed, we decided to get in the car and drive east to Watts Bar

Lake. There, we met up with the Catfish Grabblers, Marty and Fostana Jenkins, who could be described as the Instafamous noodlers of the day before there was Instagram. The Jenkinses worked in a candy factory, but on the side they filmed and produced catfish noodling videos. Their two most popular, *Girls Gone Grabblin'* and *Girls Gone Grabblin' 2*, were sold at Bass Pro Shops. Suggestive titles aside, they were family-friendly and fun to watch.

It was cold and rainy during our visit, but the Catfish Grabblers took Michelle and me out for a tour; we caught some flatheads and talked ideas. Noodling mesmerized people—those were the words Wade Bourne had used when I'd asked him about it years earlier—and as a young writer, it seemed to me there would be a way to capitalize on that. The Jenkinses sold some DVDs, but I don't think they ever struck it rich off catfish noodling.

We left Memphis to go back home to Kentucky, and we didn't starve—partly because we always had plenty of catfish to eat. And we took a lot of people noodling. We hosted outdoor television shows, some local, some national, and one from Canada. I wrote articles about noodling for Realtree, *Field & Stream*, *Fur-Fish-Game*, and other magazines. We filmed short videos for YouTube, and for a few springs we donated catfish noodling trips as fundraisers for DU banquets.

One winter a producer approached us about filming a pilot for a noodling show he was hoping to create, an offshoot of the Animal Planet reality series *Hillbilly Handfishin'*. The plan was for various noodling teams from different parts of the country to compete in an Okie Noodling–style tournament, all filmed in a reality television format. My brother, Matt, Michelle, and I would've been Team Kentucky. But we backed out, and the show launched without us. It didn't last long. Neither, for that matter, did *Hillbilly Handfishin'*—it was canceled after two seasons.

Noodling, it seemed, wasn't a mystery anymore. And so maybe people were no longer mesmerized by it.

I've seen noodling ebb and flow in popularity a few times now—enough to know that Wade was right: people *are* mesmerized by it, and I think they always will be.

A few summers ago, Ryan and I were probing the edges of a concrete flood wall, feeling for washouts underneath that might be big enough to hold a catfish. I've been fishing that wall for 20 years now; some years there are holes under it, and some years there are not. But it's always worth checking.

Ryan was still bleeding a little from a big channel cat he'd caught earlier in the day. "You know what people at work ask me, when I tell them I'm going noodling?" he said. "They ask if I'm going with Hannah. I don't know who Hannah is." Ryan is not on Facebook, Instagram, or any other social media platform and never has been. I told him about Hannah Barron and did my best to explain the logic of hashtags.

"Hashtag? What's it do?" he asked.

"I don't know. I'm not sure anyone does."

"Well. Hell."

I looked across to the johnboats, anchored in a line down the shoreline. There were three, and our crew was all in the water, sun-baked, middle-aged, and smiling. On the one hand, I was looking at engineers and teachers; art professors, HVAC technicians, soil conservation specialists, and marketing directors. On the other hand, I was looking at a hardened crowd, united by 20 summers of blood sport that never made any of us rich but had put a couple of us in the hospital. We rarely clean fish anymore. Partly because we got burned out years ago on eating flatheads. Mostly because we'd all rather catch them again than kill them.

It was searing hot, the kind of day where you splash water onto the boat seat before you climb in because the aluminum will leave grill marks on your skin if you don't. Tim and Matt were probing a spot we've long called the Hoffa Hole since it's big enough to hide a body and is the spot where we caught our first 50-pounder.

There are men and women both in our crew. Old tattoos are on display, some real ones and some scars, from catfish and C-sections. Among the men are magnificent tangles of chest hair that catch catfish slime, which dries in the sun like resin and sometimes has to be trimmed out with scissors. Middle-aged noodlers, perhaps better than anyone, know the reality of love-handle tan lines.

We're still full of it by day. Sometimes we still listen to Pantera. But there's no partying at night. We raised kids out there. There've been homes bought and sold. Career changes. Divorces. Tim's daughter, Alyssa, used to hold on to fish stringers when she was a toddler and let big flatheads pull her around in her life jacket. Now she's about to start medical school.

Anse likes to get his hands on big flatheads, even if he's outweighed by many of the fish. The other day he helped me wrestle a 20-pounder out from under a Tennessee slab rock. There were two fish in that hole, and Anse's Uncle Matt swapped spots with us to try to catch the second one. That's the same Uncle Matt, I told Anse, who was almost famous, back in the day, for nearly filming a pilot about a noodling show on Animal Planet.

I bet we have 20 more years of this in us, at least.

Chapter Six
The Trip Home

On Fly Fishing

Dave Hurteau has been my editor at *Field & Stream* for more than 15 years. In that time, we've argued about every conceivable topic: Bows. Broadheads. Rifles. Turkey calling. The qualities of a good western movie. The keeping of cats and calling them "pets." In fact, that we both simply love to antagonize and argue is the strongest glue of our friendship.

But close behind are our near-mirroring attitudes toward fishing. We both love fishing because we both love to eat fish. Hurteau has regaled me with tales of wading the Upper Delaware with a club clipped to his belt for smashing in the skulls of trophy brown trout. They have a rich flesh, he says, that's superior even to salmon. I'd fly a flag, if I had an appropriate one, to show Hurteau my support for this behavior. Me, I live on the shore of Kentucky Lake, one of the most popular tournament fisheries in the country. I love eating prize-winning largemouth bass, too, particularly when they've been flipped over the gunwale of my camouflage johnboat within eyesight of anglers in a glittering fiberglass bass boat who've paid to fish in a tournament.

On the subject of fishing, if nothing else at all, Hurteau and I have lived for years in relative harmony. So, I was disappointed when one day he said that he prefers fly fishing over spin fishing because "fly fishing is more fun."

"As proof, you never see anyone casting a spinning rod for the fun of it in a yard," he added.

I've never seen anyone cast for fun in the yard with a fly rod, either. Around here, something like that would draw a crowd of concerned neighbors to gawk and point. "The lake is more than a mile away," they'd say.

Using a fly rod proves that your motivation for casting isn't necessarily to catch a fish, and that's dumb. But if it wasn't true, there'd be no such thing as a "false cast." Why would you make a bunch of fake casts before firing your good one out there? I've watched fly anglers false cast five or six times before making the real one (a distance performance that can usually be outdone with a Snoopy pole).

Shoot, my favorite fishing days are the ones when I catch six fish on six casts. Hell, I have even more fun when I don't have to cast for them at all. Once the water gets good and warm, I'll shoot them with a bow and arrow or just jump in and wrestle them by hand. Know how many expensive rods I've broken out catfish noodling? Not a one.

Besides that, fly fishing is selfish, and that's no fun for anyone. No one else around you is allowed to fish because you need room to cast. Look, I like to reel up a big 'un while my wife and kid cheer me on, same as anyone, but asking them to sit quietly in the boat while I flail about like Zorro seems like a good way to hear some complaining—and there's no complaining quite as severe as that of a wife and kid savaging Old Dad in the confines of a boat.

Speaking of kids, show my boy a pond with a bass in it but then tell him the shoreline is too thick for casting. That kid will crawl through briars if he has to, and after a minute he'll find an opening through the willows just big enough to launch a quarter-ounce Rat-L-Trap clear to the other bank with his Zebco 33. In fact, he'll only consider the inconvenience of the thicket when he emerges back out of it and Michelle is chewing at his ass to check for ticks.

Try wielding a fly rod in that same thicket and tell me again how much fun you're having. You'll still need to check for ticks when you're done.

Hoola-Bear

I had no choice but to get out of bed, fetch a .22 pistol, and go shoot the armadillo. It was 2:00 a.m., and Levee had long since crossed over into madness, baying nonstop, which is the way he gets when he's found an armadillo in the middle of the night.

Levee is a Catahoula leopard dog, overweight but handsome, and a terrible animal by all objective measures. I knew that I could stand on the porch and scream at him, plead with him, to shut up. I could buzz him with a shock collar or wade off into the darkness with a stick to beat him. None of it would make any difference. Sometimes I believe that Levee dreams of nothing except catching and killing 9-banded armadillos. I've always kind of wondered what he'd be like around a wild hog.

That's what Catahoulas are mostly bred for after all: hog hunting. They're the state dog of Louisiana, and legend has it that the earliest ones were the result of interbreeding among Native American dogs and red wolves. Michelle simply had to have one after a hog hunt in South Florida years ago. One of the dogs in the pack we followed was a giant blue merle named Thor. Catahoulas are typically bay dogs, but Thor was a catch dog, the one that rushes in and chomps down on an enraged wild boar's face, holding it in place long enough so that you can kill it with a knife. Thor's owner warned us not to be fooled by the dog's good looks. "I wouldn't recommend that anybody get a Catahoula," he said.

Indeed, the National Association of Louisiana Catahoulas has an official motto: Not everyone needs a Catahoula. Catahoula lore says that you must actually be gifted one in order to own one. Some of that lore has changed, though; most reputable Catahoula breeders expect $700 or more cash before "gifting" you a puppy. But they are selective in who they'll sell to, requiring prospective owners to submit a résumé of sorts to prove that the dogs are going to an outdoorsy home with the space to contain them and, ideally, will have a job to do.

We wanted a blood-tracking dog and a loyal protector. And so, we got Levee. Anse was two years old when we brought the puppy home, and the two of them became fast and rowdy buddies that Michelle and I collectively dubbed "The Boys."

As a trainer, I'm sure that I messed up with Levee right out of the gate. I simply don't have the patience to be a good dog trainer, particularly with a dog as independent and hardheaded as Levee rapidly proved himself to be. I worked with him some in the evenings, setting up fake trails with deer blood I'd put in the freezer, and he seemed to catch on quickly. So, when he was seven months old, I put him on his first real track—a heart-shot doe that I watched fall dead from the stand—and Levee found the animal in less than 30 seconds. I field-dressed the deer and tossed him a little chunk of flank meat for the reward. This is easy enough, I thought.

During that deer season and the next one, Levee seemed to hit his stride as a tracking dog, too, finding one deer after the next. I even wrote a story about tracking dogs for *Field & Stream*, and his photograph appeared in the table of contents. At home, he went through a dog-loving family's typical progression of nicknames. He has at times been Levee, Lev-O, Houla, Hoolie, Hoola-Bear, and Big Red Bastard. Good as he was at tracking, he seemed to excel at another job—being by young Anse Brantley's side at all times, where he has been unfailingly gentle and loving but also fiercely protective.

But as Levee matured, he became increasingly difficult to deal with in the deer woods. His immense strength made holding him on a 20-foot lead a challenge, particularly when he was ripping through a blackberry thicket. He found deer easily enough but would often growl at me when he did as soon as I moved in to take possession. We had him neutered, and that settled him down—but then he absolutely would not load back into his dog box.

All the while, I realized that tracking was cutting into my hunting. Many of the really good trackers I know don't even deer hunt themselves. They're dog people, in other words, and God bless them for being there. Me, I'd rather hunt. So, Levee and I retired from blood trails.

Anse told his grandparents, "Levee got mean, so we cut his two balls off, and now he's just fat." And he's not wrong. Hoola-Bear enjoys table scraps and sleeping in the sun above all else, and now, he's eight years old, with a gray muzzle.

But he is still damn good at catching armadillos.

I walked off the porch in my gym shorts and Crocs, a Streamlight in one hand and Smith & Wesson in the other. Levee's barks and snarls on the hillside harkened back to caught pigs in the palmettos, long spears, and a blue merle named Thor, and I thought, "You'd have been good at that, too, you Big Red Bastard."

I shined the light on him, and a pair of blood red eyes shown back, a sight that would've been straight out of a nightmare if I hadn't known the dog was grinning wildly underneath. "What you got, buddy?!" I yelled in a childlike voice. He yipped and dug at the armadillo with his front paws, but you'd have needed a backhoe to dislodge the creature so long as it was breathing. I suspected this particular varmint was the same one that had been digging holes in the yard, and besides that, I was ready to go back to bed. The .22 cracked in the darkness, and the barking stopped, although I could hear massive jaws, a catch dog's jaws, crushing the shell out in the brush.

The armadillo was laying on the back patio the next morning, smashed in and bloodied, and Levee was stretched out on his back on the living room floor, feet pointed at the ceiling and his jowls sagging in a goofy grin. Anse was laying on the ground next to the dog, revving him up to wrestle. Michelle was on the couch with a cup of coffee, smiling at The Boys.

BEAVERCUE

Anse and I smelled like Hell Fire predator lure, and Michelle wouldn't let us into the cabin until we left our coats and coveralls on the porch. Anse, at age seven, wormed out of his Carhartts and giggled "Hell Fire" over and over again until Michelle got after him for his cussing.

"It doesn't count, Mama, because that's the name of the lure!" he said, and then he looked at me for support.

"Quit cussing," I said.

Hell Fire is a gelled predator attractant that smells pungently of skunk and is sold in a tiny glass bottle. In trapper's lingo, the smell is "loud." I won't touch a jar of it without rubber gloves, and I only apply the lure to the grass near a finished set with a stick. Anse got hold of one of those sticks, swung it around like a sword, and ended up with a good smear of Hell Fire across the chest of his coveralls. You could smell him from 30 yards for the rest of trapping season.

I used to dread the off-season between the end of deer hunting and the beginning of spring turkey hunting. But then Anse and I got into trapping. Now we spend that off-season time making land sets for coyotes, raccoons, foxes, and bobcats and water sets for beaver, otters, muskrats, and minks. We've had better turkey hatches on our place every year since we started predator trapping, and that was the primary goal. But we've also come to love the season and the process itself. I skin and sell some of the raw furs and give Anse the few dollars we make for his piggy bank. We spend far more than that sending the prettier stuff off to be tanned and returned to keep for ourselves or give away as gifts to friends. Michelle says she'd like to learn to flesh and soft-tan our furs herself, but for now, that's just an aspiration.

Trapping teaches you a lot about using scents. Everything about the process has a distinct smell. Inside the cabin was a better odor, one of slow-cooking meat not unlike that of a beef roast. I lifted the Crock-Pot lid and seined away some of the fat that had been rendered from the quarters bubbling in a stock of Coors Light, beef broth, onions, and seasonings. I pulled at the meat—rich and greasy—and discarded the bones.

"The porch smells like a skunk, and the whole cabin smells like a damn beaver!" Michelle said. Anse had stripped down to his white cotton long johns, the kind old men wear, and turned on *Wild Kratts*.

"Look here, buddy," I said, holding up a bag of King's Hawaiian sweet rolls in one hand and a brand-new bottle of Sweet Baby Ray's barbecue sauce in the other. "How about some beavercue sliders and Tater Tots for lunch?"

Anse swooned dramatically and said, "Beavercuuue," drawing out the word as if eating the sandwiches would relieve him of some great burden he'd been carrying for days.

I know hunters who are uncomfortable with trapping because they don't like the idea of killing an animal without eating it. Generally, I'm of that mindset too. But there are limits. I've seen the virtue-signaling videos of people cooking and eating coyotes, for example, and carrying on as if they've done something really noble. But I've watched turkey vultures ignore skinned coyotes. Personally, I can avoid eating anything a buzzard won't touch and still sleep okay.

But show me a nice beaver killed clean by a 330 Conibear and held overnight in ice water, and I'll show you the beginning of a good feed—plus a nice fur to boot. Beavers are obese vegetarians (an oxymoron, like jumbo shrimp) and the world's second-biggest rodent species. The biggest is the capybara, a South American critter that also lives in the water and is equally delicious. I killed one once in Argentina with a nice Benelli shotgun and a makeshift load of buckshot made from steel ball bearings, guided by a man named Cally who spoke no English.

Insulating fat and a clean diet give beavers a flavor that's often compared to that of beef. Bullfrogs and squirrels are said to taste like chicken, but they don't at all. But a slow-cooked beaver really does taste like roast beef. Anse likes his best soaked in barbecue sauce and served on a sweet roll.

Beavercue sliders are not Michelle's favorite food. Anse, with sauce already staining his long johns, knew this and would not miss a chance to do some virtue signaling of his own. "Mama, you need to get a plate and eat some of this damn beaver," he said. Then he looked at me. "It's not a cuss word, right, because of beaver dams? And Mama said it earlier, too."

Michelle put a tiny scoop of beavercue on a single Hawaiian roll and sat down next to Anse. I've watched her handle a snake—despite being terrified of it—purely to teach Anse that irrational fear is silly. "The damn beavers do build beaver dams," she said to him. "But I'm still going to whip your ass if you keep up that cussing."

I used to hate those short, cold days of late winter. But now, with the trapping and the beavercue and the cussing, it's become one of my favorite times of the year.

Trout Bums

Michelle seemed almost ashamed when I told her I'd like to go trout fishing, as if I'd also suggested that we get a cat. She and Anse love to fish, but the idea of burning summer vacation days to catch and release 8-ounce trout that are too fancy to fillet didn't sit well. She suggested we go to Gulf Shores instead, where we could bowfish for stingrays.

But I dug my heels in on trout. Not that I had any intention of going to Montana or of buying waders that weren't camouflaged. No, what we'd do is tow my johnboat to Arkansas and fish for trout stocked from a truck, with spinning rods and Rebel Crawdads. We'd eat them, too.

Trout aren't native to Arkansas, but they have been stocked in the cold tailwaters below several Corps of Engineers Lakes including Bull Shoals on the White River and Greers Ferry on the Little Red. Although the rainbow trout aren't self-sustaining and must be continually restocked, the brown trout are able to spawn successfully in some of the tailwater fisheries. In fact, the Little Red is home to one of history's largest browns, a 40-pound, 4-ounce behemoth caught in 1992.

The little bit of trout fishing I've done in my life was mostly on the White River, nearly 30 years ago, when I was just a little older than Anse. I went with my dad and his buddy Kenny Dean, and we drifted with the current, casting crankbaits at the bank. Once, I remember a big brown trout, easy to see in the clear water, that emerged from under a root wad and followed my crawdad to the boat and then spun away in a flash of gold without biting. That was the closest I ever got to catching one.

Maybe the promise of a nice brown was part of the reason why I insisted on the trout trip. Michelle and Anse finally agreed to go. We rented a cottage on the water and launched my boat at daybreak into a cold, heavy fog, rendered by frigid tailwater hitting the humid summer air. Michelle, having packed for summer in Arkansas, wrapped herself in a beach towel and shivered, while Anse side-eyed the rainbow trout–colored Rapala Minnow I had tied to his rod.

"Why would they eat their own kind?" he asked.

"I think it's because trout are stupid," Michelle said.

I'd promised nonstop action from stocker rainbows—that's what I remembered as a kid—but it wasn't happening. We fished and floated and said little, and after two fishless hours, I could sense mutiny in the air. I cast a white X-Rap at the bank and ripped it back; slash, slash, pause. Nothing. Anse threw the trout-colored Rapala. Michelle worked a red and gold Little Cleo. The monotony of not catching fish was only broken occasionally to pull grass off hooks or to turn the boat and plow back upstream, with the trolling motor on full power, to free snagged plugs from boat docks. Truthfully, I've had more fun at work.

We passed a drift boat of fly anglers, all of whom were wearing straw hats and brightly colored long sleeves. One of them was fighting a nice trout.

"Deeds, looks like they're using bobbers and worms," Anse said, hope in his voice. We had a whole box of bream tackle with us.

"Shh, those are strike indicators, buddy, not bobbers. I'm sure they have tiny nymphs under them," I said.

Michelle looked as though she might never smile again.

Anse made another cast, this time landing the bright crankbait just off the edge of a riprapped shoreline. He twitched it once, and his rod suddenly bowed under the heft of a twisting stocker rainbow. "Oh, buddy, you've got one!" I yelled, dropping my own rod and scrambling for the net. But the trout shook loose 6 feet from the boat.

Anse slowly reeled in the empty crankbait, stood quietly for a moment, and then said, "That fruity bastard." The fly anglers in the drift boat looked at us and furrowed their brows, as if children from Arkansas never cuss.

"It's okay, buddy, throw another cast," I coached. The disappointment didn't last long, as that strike was an omen of a hot bite to come. Anse landed his first trout only a few casts later, and then Michelle caught one, too. Soon, our ice chest was thumping with thrashing trout, and I stood on the bow of the boat, soaking up the admiration due to a good fishing guide.

"Deeds, two more and I'll have my limit!" Anse said, and by then we were being picky, releasing small rainbows one after another. When we drifted past a current break behind a big root wad, I fired the X-Rap toward the shore, twitched it twice, and felt a decisively heavier strike on the other end. "Ooh, good one!" I said, loud and deep, to ensure that anyone doing yard work on the bank could take the time to stop what they were doing and watch the fight properly.

"Deeds, can I reel it in?" Anse begged, reaching for my rod, but I pulled it away.

"Hell no, this is my fish, but you can get the net!" My drag buzzed, and I turned the boat away from shore with the trolling motor to fight the trout over open water. Soon, Anse scooped the brown into the net, but Michelle had to threaten him with a spanking before he'd pose for a picture with it, and even then he wouldn't smile.

"I've wanted to catch a trout like this since I was his age," I said, admiring my prize.

"It's only because you've got that fancy white crankbait," Anse huffed.

"Put that thing in the cooler," Michelle said.

But that didn't feel right to me, and so, with mutiny again in the air, I eased the brown trout back into the water and watched it dart away toward the root wad. Then I tied another white X-Rap to Anse's rod.

Five minutes later, a bigger brown followed my lure from underneath a dock and smashed it at the side of the boat, a vicious strike rivaling that of any smallmouth bass. I carefully fought the trout to the boat and netted it. It was near 20 inches long, thick and meaty.

"You know, we get one of these big ones per day, per person in the creel limit," I said out loud, mostly to myself, although Michelle heard it because she opened the cooler.

The stocker rainbow trout we ate that night, wrapped in foil and grilled whole, were good. But the rich flesh of the brown trout, sautéed in a skillet with butter and garlic salt, was as fine as any fish I've eaten. It was certainly worth a few days of summer vacation—and even good enough to make trout bums out of us all.

Lake Locals

In my dream, I'm on the deck of a camouflage johnboat that's sitting idle on a mudflat, having succumbed to an outboard motor that won't start. In the floor of the boat is an open tool box, a broken fishing rod, a bow and arrow, a .22 rifle, and an empty fried chicken bucket. Since it's a dream, some of it seems weird; I am, for example, juggling a carp, a catfish, and a dead squirrel. And there's a videographer, wearing sodden skinny jeans and squatting in the

Skinning Catfish in Mary's Kitchen

mud, holding a GoPro and asking if I could maybe toss the catfish a bit higher and wondering aloud when I'll have the motor fixed so we can go bluegill fishing, throw some poppers for bass, and toss out a spread of teal decoys.

I can't juggle in real life, but I do it furiously in the dream. The squirrel's fur becomes matted in catfish slime, the carp gets stiff and rancid, and the videographer complains about it being hot. In the open water behind me, a wake boat attempts to put a large woman up onto skis, but she falters and skips across the surface like a flat rock, even though not one part of her is the least bit flat.

And all the while I'm juggling and smiling because there's nowhere in the world I'd rather be than on Kentucky Lake, sorting out a mess just like this one. It's a vacation destination with a summer tourist season, but we live here year-round, Michelle, Anse, and I, because there's something to do outside during all 12 months. We hunt squirrels and deer in the fall and ducks all winter. Come spring we fish for bass and crappie and shellcrackers but while wearing full camo and with shotguns handy because, sometimes, we hear turkeys gobble up on the bank. In the summer we wrestle flathead catfish from underneath rocks and bowfish for carp and gig frogs and run limblines. Some evenings, when Anse was little, I'd pull my four-wheeler down to the bank, and he'd jump into the water and pretend to be a Mosasaurus.

We've hosted so many guests in the summer that Michelle says our place is like a halfway house for rednecks. Quite a few out-of-towners come here to film catfish noodling and bowfishing with us for outdoor television shows and their YouTube channels, and some of them get a full taste of local lake life while they're here. One summer, a crew from Nashville had joined us, and as we were cruising up the main river channel, we spotted a pontoon boat that had run aground on a steep, red-clay bank.

We motored up to help, and a drunk man and woman were out on the bank, standing in the mud and pushing the pontoon, which would not budge. They'd been running up the river full throttle, drinking beer and having sex, all at once, when they lost control and crashed the boat. We didn't see or catch any of that on film, but it was the very first thing the couple told us. I could tell they were proud of it and, despite the inconvenience of the beached boat, would do it all over again as soon as they could, maybe even that day.

Tim was there in his boat as well, and so the two of us hooked tow ropes to the pontoon and to our johnboats and then pulled it off the bank. The drunk man raised both arms and smiled, as if he were wearing a cape, but then he slipped and fell into the mud, backward and head somehow downhill. He slid all the way to the water's edge but quickly righted himself and staggered onto the pontoon. The woman slapped him on the butt cheek and declared to everyone that, even if she'd brought a cake spatula, she "couldn't have packed mud into the crack of his ass any tighter."

That couple's problem was the same one everyone has on the lake, and it's why I warn all of my guests that the idea of a slow, Southern lifestyle is a pure myth; the pace of this place will kill you if you let it. We're going to grab catfish and shoot carp and squirrel hunt, too. If that doesn't work out, we'll try some bluegill fishing or throw some poppers for bass, and if teal season's in, we might even bring a dozen decoys with us. But we can't do it all in one day.

A lake local knows to account for the time it takes to eat some fried chicken, work on a broken boat motor, film cutaways with a GoPro, assist fellow locals stuck on the bank, and maybe take his wife on a nice evening boat ride, just the two of them. But trying to juggle too much fun at once can get the best of you—or at least cause some strange dreams.

On Gates
The two-panel gate latches shut in the middle of a cattle guard and is buttressed on both ends by 12-inch iron posts, both of which are

filled with concrete. There are holes cut in the center bar of the cattle guard, and into those go a pair of bolt-action–like latches, one for each gate panel. The latches are made of welded steel and are heavy enough to mash a thumbnail. Once the gate panels are latched to the cattle guard, they're then secured together by a cross latch and further still by a logging chain that's held together with a combination lock the size of a horse hoof. Cattle often linger just behind the gate, and they seem entertained by watching people try to open it.

Perhaps there are gates like this in places other than Texas, but perhaps not. This one is definitely in Texas. There's a high-fenced ranch full of black bucks and fallow deer just across the road. I'm a member of a hunting lease on the low-fenced property, behind the gate, and when I joined a few years back, Miles, who'd been a member for a while, took me for a drive around the place. He pulled up to the gate and waited for me to step out and open it.

I undid the combination lock easily enough, but I didn't realize that to actually open the gate, you had to pull up both vertical latches and rest them over the tops of the panels, swing the gate slightly inward, lift the left panel with one hand, undo the cross latch with the other, lower the left panel, and then swing both panels back open the other way. It must all be done in perfect synchronization, too, because if it isn't, you can't open the gate, and the cattle will see—and maybe the fallow deer across the road, too, if they're standing next to the high fence.

I pulled at bars and latches and cussed until, finally, Miles stepped out of the driver's seat of his pickup, straightened his jeans, and walked up to help.

"Well, I think it's obvious which of us grew up on a hobby farm and which of us grew up on a ranch," he said as he opened the gate. It took more than a year before he admitted that the landowner himself had shown him the correct procedure for opening and closing the gate.

The Trip Home

Spend any time out hunting or fishing, and you're going to have to go through some gates. Etiquette says that if you're riding shotgun, you're in charge of opening and closing any and all of the gates encountered throughout the day. Some gates are physically difficult to open and close, some are mentally perplexing, and a few are both. If you're on gate duty, it doesn't matter what type of gate you encounter. It's your job to open it quickly, usher the vehicle through, and then close it just as quickly, taking care to latch it exactly as it was latched previously—and to do all that without locking yourself on the wrong side of the gate.

The secret to opening and closing gates properly is realizing that there is no secret at all. Enter "types of farm gates" in Google, and you can tell that the results were curated by people who work for Google and don't spend much time opening and closing farm gates. When a gate is difficult to open, it's usually because some tension needs to be taken off a latch or wire. Doing that might require releasing some special tensioner that was fashioned by cowboys on the spot, but most of the time it just takes muscle. When you're on gate duty, you get to show everyone, even the cattle, that you're either strong enough to sit in the front seat or you're not.

Of course, managing a bad gate successfully can make you feel like a conquistador. A few seasons ago, Ryan and I hired a packer with a team of horses and mules to get us out of a backcountry elk camp. It was sunny and warm when we saddled up but snowing sideways a couple miles down the trail. We came to a cedar-post-and-barbed-wire gate, held against the fence by two rusted loops of wire. I dismounted and pushed on the post and up on the wire, which was strung so tight that it was actually dug into the wood.

My boots slid in the mud against the post, but the wire wouldn't budge. I could tell that Ryan and the packer were thinking of dismounting, and I knew embarrassment was only moments away. I quickly stepped behind a fence post and braced myself against it, which gave me just enough leverage to pull the gate post toward me and pop the wire loose. Half the fence collapsed, and the horses clopped through, farting as horses often do.

"Man, that gate looked like a booger," Ryan said as I wired it back shut.

"Wasn't that bad," I replied, swinging a leg over the saddle.

"The old man with the grazing rights up here comes through that gate every day to check his cows. He's probably 80," the packer said. "Opens it with one hand."

The navigator, whether he's on the lead horse or in the driver's seat of a pickup, has a job, too, and that's to always keep the gate man in his place.

Born-Again Duck Hunter

A few years ago, I almost quit duck hunting. It was a gradual slide that began with storing my decoys in Ryan's barn while Michelle and I were between houses. That fall, I bought my duck stamp and filled out my HIP survey with all the usual intentions. But then I skipped the Thanksgiving opener and most of December. Meanwhile, my decoys sat in that barn, in the rafters above a horse stall, gathering dust. And I'll tell you, horses are dusty animals.

Ten years ago, if you'd told me this was coming, I'd have said you were crazy because duck hunting is one of my favorites, just behind chasing spring gobblers and bowhunting whitetails. I've hunted ducks and geese in every flyway of the United States, in three Canadian provinces, and twice in Argentina. Used to be that if I hunted fewer than 30 days of our 60-day season, I thought I was half-assing it.

But 10 years ago, Anse wasn't around. He has the same compulsion to be in the woods that I do. He shot his first deer when he was six and his first gobbler the following spring. So, when it came to waterfowl hunting, it was a struggle for me to walk out the door to hunt by myself when he was begging to go with me.

The Trip Home

Why didn't I just take him duck hunting? Because I have little interest in sitting in a blind with a propane heater. Where I want to be is in my boat on a big river, waiting for snot to freeze while I look for ducks and scheme on places to hide. That type of hunting is dangerous. Michelle, who spent years in the boat hunting with me, knows the realities of hunting big water in the winter. For a long time, we both agreed that Anse was too young for it. I guess that's why I hit the pause button on duck hunting, and I told myself I didn't even really miss it.

We drove to our hunting lease in central Texas the day after Christmas. It's become a winter vacation tradition for us, going to Texas—cheaper than Disney and more sensical, too, since we're not a family fit for the Magic Kingdom. We'd been on the lease for a few years, and most of the hunting, as you'd expect, was for deer and hogs out of shooting houses.

But that year, I decided to take a shotgun and waders, too. There are miles of wild country between the deer stands, including dozens of stock ponds, most of which are about an acre in size, with an earthen dam on one end and a shallow, muddy flat on the other. Locals call them tanks, and they're built for watering livestock, but many of them are gin clear and full of milfoil, flooded cockleburs, and all sorts of tiny, slithering critters. It's surprisingly ducky water in the middle of otherwise arid cattle country.

Where the ducks even come from adds to the mystery. Unlike in the Dakotas or the Mississippi River drainage or the Canadian prairie, you rarely look to the central Texas sky and see migrating waterfowl trading back and forth. But in the winter, especially after a heavy rain, they simply show up: gadwalls, greenwings, pintails, and wigeon, loafing and preening their full plumage on virtually any depression deep enough to puddle water. Most tanks will at least have a couple ducks sitting on them.

And so, after dropping Michelle off at a deer stand before daybreak, Anse and I took a walk. I carried my 20-gauge and two pockets of shells. We snuck around the low side of the first tank, below the dam so as to stay out of sight, and then belly-crawled to the rim of it, where cattle had beaten a path to fine dirt. "Peek over the top and see if you see any ducks," I whispered to Anse. He stood slowly and then crouched back immediately, as if he was expecting enemy fire.

"Deeds, there are three greenhead mallards sitting right there!" he whispered.

I readied the shotgun and said, "Well, stand up and scare the shit out of them for me."

Anse is pretty good at being quiet if he thinks it's required for shooting something, but he would much rather cause a ruckus, especially with my blessing. He stood and yelled, "Get outta here, birds!," and a dozen mallards boiled off the tank at our feet. I shouldered the gun and dropped a greenhead with the first shot, missed the second, and then killed another drake with the final shell.

Both ducks were laying on the shallow flat, where the sound and smell of the muck could've been from Canada or the Dakotas or perhaps the riverbank back home. "Look at how *big* they are," Anse said, and I was struck by the colors, as I always am. Common as they are, not much in nature looks better than a big drake mallard.

We bagged a pair of gadwalls from the next tank and two more from a puddle after that. Anse shot at a shoveler, but my shotgun was too long for him and kicked too much, he said, and besides, he was having a great time crawling across cow pastures just to flush them. We stopped at my limit and called it a good morning, but before cleaning birds, we decided to scout a couple more tanks to hunt the next morning. One of them had 30 or 40 ducks sitting on it, just 20 yards from a giant cluster of willow bushes. We looked them over and then quietly snuck back out of sight.

"You're going to see something special in the morning," I told him.

We dropped Michelle off at her deer stand early that next day, giving Anse and me enough time to toss out a few decoys and cut out a place to hide in the willow bushes. I sipped coffee as the sky softened, and wings whistled and ripped above us. Gadwalls and teal splashed at our feet and chirped and quacked and whistled. "Look at all of them," Anse whispered, knowing it was a time to be quiet.

"You just keep handing me shells once the shooting starts," I said.

I'd set an alarm on my phone to buzz in my pocket at legal light, anticipating that very situation. The ducks erupted into glorious chaos, circled the tank, and dropped back on top of us. I didn't need my duck call, but I used it, dropping it at my neck at the last second to shoulder on cupped birds over decoys, the jingle of old bands cut off by shotgun blasts and the slap of birds hitting the water.

Duck hunting was just as good as I remembered it, except for the boy's smile, a new thing that made it all even better.

Purpose Point

I don't mind going camping if it's for a purpose. I've spent collective months of my life sleeping in tents and on the ground because it's been required to reach the critters I'm hunting. But as a result of all that camping, I've decided that if given the choice, a cabin with a bed and a stove beats a sleeping bag in the rocks and a Jet-Boil every single time.

But one summer Anse wanted to go camping. He'd been hunting, fishing, trapping, and generally bumming around with me in the woods since he could walk—but he'd never slept a night outside, on the ground. I figured that at his age it was time for some new life lessons, including that going camping just for the hell of it is miserable.

We had a forecast stretch of three 80-degree days in early June, which is about as pleasant as it gets in southern Kentucky in the summer. Anse and I loaded my johnboat with a two-person tent, sleeping bags, fire grate, and a few other primitive camp essentials. The kid, who's a fan of *Alone* and *Naked and Afraid*, insisted that we depend solely on the river and the land to feed us. Unlike contestants on the shows, though, we could bring along whatever gear we wanted. And so, we brought spinning rods and jigs and nightcrawlers and bowfishing rigs, limblines, a frog gig, a .22 pistol, and a whole sleeve of CCI Stingers. Although I kept it secret, I also stashed some emergency rations, including chocolate and marshmallows, in the dry bag, just in case.

We launched late in the afternoon and ran south for a few miles, crossing the Tennessee River channel and then beaching on a gravel point with a calm, protected pocket on the lee side. We set up camp just inside the trees, under the shade of a hickory but still on the gravel, and gathered a few large rocks to build a fire ring. After that, with only a few hours of daylight left, I told Anse we better get to work catching dinner.

The same cold front that had made for tolerable weather also created tough fishing. We started out casting for white bass that we'd seen chasing schools of shad. When that didn't work, I put a worm on a drop-shot rig and caught a keeper bluegill my first cast—and then we didn't get another peck. Under normal circumstances, Anse can make it maybe 45 minutes without eating anything at all, and he expects a full supper at about 6:00 p.m. That evening, the shadows were getting longer, and lunch from earlier in the day was a distant memory. I asked Anse if he was hungry, and he said "no." But I knew better and could tell he was worried about sleeping on the ground with an empty gut. He fired another cast with a curly-tail and reeled it in slowly. Nothing.

But we were fishing in a familiar bay, and I knew of a particular rock up in the shallows with a washout underneath it. I'd wrestled flathead catfish out from under it before. "Boy, you want to drop an anchor and see if we can grab a flathead out from under that rock?"

I asked. Anse nodded, wild-eyed and predatory. He stashed his rod, shucked off his shirt, and jumped into the water. I jumped in as well, and soon we were both lying in the water on our stomachs at the edge of the rock.

"You think there's one in there, Deeds?" Anse whispered, as if a catfish might hear him.

"Probably is," I said. "Be ready."

I took a breath, dropped below the surface, and slithered my arm into the hole, all the way up to my shoulder, and it was like a grenade went off inside. A flathead hit me with a vicious bite that engulfed my entire hand. I grabbed the fish's jaw before it could let go, squeezed hard as I could, and began pulling it to me. The fish shook its head as I pulled it to the front of the hole, like a bass trying to lose a crankbait, and my knuckles were paying the price. But this was dinner, and I knew better than to let go.

The water was shallow enough that I could get my face to the surface, sputter for a breath, and yell for Anse to get a stringer. "Hang on to him, Deeds!" he yelled, and I saw a braided yellow rope unfurl. Back underwater I worked a second hand into the fight, under a gill plate, but I wasn't alone. The kid's bony arms worked in tandem with my own, carefully guiding the point of the stringer through the fish's mouth, out the gill plate, and then back to the surface. Anse and I pulled the fish out together, and he wrapped the stringer around his arm a few turns and ran for the bank, dragging behind him a fish that was a third his body size in a melee of mud and slime.

"We got enough for dinner now and breakfast, too, Deeds!" he yelled. I knew he was under the illusion that we'd be smoking the fish on green sticks without any salt, and so I figured it was time to fess up about the extra food I'd packed.

"Guess what I snuck into the dry bag?" I asked. He shrugged. "A skillet, some oil, fish batter, a can of beans, some instant mashed taters, and s'mores. You sure you're not hungry?"

He smiled as if I'd also revealed to him that school was canceled indefinitely.

We built a hot fire with driftwood and cleaned the catfish over a log, with Anse holding it by the jaw as I trimmed away the fillets and belly meat, which we planned to cook for dinner. The rest of the fish went into the cooler. I unfolded a cooking grate and set an 8-inch iron skillet over the top of it to heat. Anse built a pyramid of kindling, but I told him that I'd handle the cooking if he wanted to get a few casts in before dark. He grabbed a spinning rod and worked his way around the point and out of sight.

I fried the catfish to golden brown a few pieces at a time, adjusting the skillet over the coals as needed to keep the oil sizzling but not smoking. Instant potatoes and a can of beans bubbled around the edges, with just enough daylight to see it all cooking and a lake breeze just steady enough to carry the smell of a fish fry down the point. Anse came walking back into camp as sure as if a dinner bell had been rung, and he sat on a large rock to eat his catfish. We cleaned up supper, stoked the fire, watched the sun fade over the water, and, when it got plenty dark, eased around the calm pocket with the trolling motor to gig frogs. It was only after the day's second round of blood and slime was washed away that we finally settled into our sleeping bags. "Hey, Deeds," Anse said in the dark. "Will we be able to come back here one day? Camping was awesome."

Of course it was. We hadn't gone out there with a purpose, but we sure found one. That night, on a bed of gravel, I slept soundly.

The Thrash-Metal Turkey

Michelle and I bought Anse tickets to a Metallica concert for Christmas, a gift that was as much for us as it was for him. The show was the first weekend in May, coincidentally the last weekend of turkey season. Usually, Tim and I leave for Nebraska that weekend, but that spring, neither of us drew tags.

The Trip Home

I thought I'd be okay to just let turkey season end and be content with what had already been a good year. We'd started hunting turkeys in late March down in Texas, then on to Tennessee and Kentucky. We'd shot plenty of gobblers, and as the end of the season neared, Anse declared that he was "good on turkeys for the year," even though he still had a Kentucky tag left. I oiled my shotgun and put my calls away, and even though it all seemed premature, I accepted it.

"It's kind of relaxing, knowing that I don't have to pack again and leave for another trip," I said to Michelle one evening. "We can go to our concert and enjoy it and then just come on back home. Shellcrackers will be biting, and y'all will be finishing up school. I can live without shooting another turkey."

But then my buddy Jason Gilbertson texted at almost that very moment, as if he'd been listening to a hidden recorder and couldn't stomach the lies for one second longer. Gilbertson, who works for Winchester Ammunition, asked if I could be in Michigan that Sunday to hunt gobblers with their new Longbeard TSS turkey load. I told him that I absolutely could not—but that I could probably be there by Monday.

I pulled my gun back out of the safe, then loaded my truck with all my camo, calls, and hunting gear and made plans to jump in and head north to Michigan as soon as we got home from the Metallica concert.

We were groggy that morning, even though we'd done our best to get moving. We'd rushed to the parking lot the night before as soon as the "Enter Sandman" finale was over. Tim had joined us for the concert, and we all shared a motel room a few miles from the stadium. At 2:00 a.m., having finally crashed from the endorphins of steel guitars and several boxes of candy, Anse fell into a deep slumber in the floor at the foot of my and Michelle's bed. I felt guilty, waking him so early after daybreak, but I had to get back on the road, up to Michigan.

"Deeds, are you turkey hunting again?" Anse asked as we got closer to home. I told him that I was. "When does the season go out here?"

"Buddy, today is the last day."

"Wait, but I still have a tag left!" he said in protest. I reminded him that he'd already said he was "good on turkeys for the year" and that he'd have to wait until next spring to hunt another one. But then we pulled into the driveway, and a longbeard gobbler was strutting in the backyard, next to Anse's treehouse.

All of my hunting gear was packed in my truck, and I couldn't get to it without scaring the gobbler, which was displaying in earnest for three hens that were picking at bugs in our yard. But I was wearing a pair of brown Carhartt pants and a green sweatshirt—camo enough, I figured, if I sat still. Michelle fished a camo mask out of a drawer and tossed it to me. Anse had already changed into his gear faster than Clark Kent in a phone booth and was urging me to hurry up. He handed me a glass call from his turkey pouch, loaded his 20-gauge, and said, "Let's go get him, Deeds."

We snuck out the front door, with Michelle, Tim, and Levee, our dog, watching the show from the kitchen window. The Kentucky turkey season was near over but not yet. Anse and I crouched behind the garage to cut some distance between ourselves and the birds and then belly-crawled into a good position near the treehouse, behind a tangle of privet. We could see the gobbler puffing and spinning through the privet stalks, not 50 yards away. All we needed to do was get him to step out into the yard for a good, open shot.

Anse rested his gun on his knee, and I lay prone on the ground behind him with the glass call. Despite the dozens of turkeys we'd worked already that spring and despite all of the hundreds of turkeys I'd worked in the years before, my knuckles still trembled with anticipation as I scratched the first cluck out of the call. The tom's white head snapped behind the privet, and its gobble was so loud that it seemed to shake the ground under my belly.

"Safety off, get ready," I whispered to Anse. The turkey gobbled again and stepped closer, drumming, a soft hum that you seem to hear through your molars as much as your ears. The bird gobbled again, and I was looking up at it, through the crook of Anse's arm and elbow, where his right hand was holding steady and still on the grip of the shotgun. But to freeze that moment in time.

The gobbler was just 10 yards away now, a brilliant sight but still behind the privet, as if he knew better than to step farther out into the open. Suddenly the turkey extended its neck and its fan unfurled, and then it lifted and tucked a wing and spun away from us rapidly, stepping behind the privet, its head now a blistering blood red. It was spooked and trying to get away quickly. The gobbler stepped into view once more, for just a moment, trotting across the open yard in front of the treehouse, 35 yards away.

As it hit a dead run, Anse Brantley spun, shouldered his gun, leaned out away from the privet, and shot the tom dead. The kid put on his safety and sprang to his feet, and then he stopped again, ready to shoot if needed, but it wasn't. When I reached the boy and hugged him, he had his boot across the gobbler's neck, his gun broken open and safe, holding the smoking hull in his hand.

"I thought he was going to get away," he said.

"I didn't. Good shot, buddy."

I texted Jason, my buddy with Winchester, and told him that I'd be even later than planned getting to Michigan, but for good reason. We took photos of Anse's last-day turkey while wearing our concert shirts, and when the breast was picked clean, the legs and thighs were washed and soaking in salt water, the fan was stretched and salted and pinned, and the beards and spurs were hanging, I hugged my family and said, "Well, I'm headed to Michigan now. But if I get one early, I'll come home early."

And I did get one early. But my route home took me through Indiana, and from my truck window, I saw turkeys. I called Michelle and told her I might take one more day, see what an Indiana license costs, and drive a few new back roads to see if I could round up another story or two to tell before hunting season ended and I finished the trip home.

Afterword and Acknowledgments

Mary Francis Adams, my late mother-in-law, never got to read this collection in its entirety, but she did get to read "Skinning Catfish in Mary's Kitchen," an essay I submitted to the *Field & Stream* website and dedicated to Mary on Mother's Day back in 2023.

Mary was diagnosed with terminal cancer about a month after I turned in the first draft of this book. She passed away just three days later. Everyone was sad except for Mary, who said she was ready to go and be with Larry, and who cracked jokes right up until her final moments. She also asked, with labored breath, if I planned on naming my book after her. I told her that I was. Mary was the librarian in Dawson Springs for more than 30 years, and she loved a good book. I'd like to think she would've enjoyed this one, although she'd have probably gotten after me for including too much cussing.

I've enjoyed a perfect career. I've been gainfully employed a few times on various editorial staffs, but I've made my living primarily as a full-time freelance writer and editor. I've had bylines in many different publications, but a few in particular stand out. I've written hundreds of stories and edited many thousands more for Realtree.com, the website for Bill Jordan's Realtree Camouflage. Some of those stories are in this book, including *On BB Gun Safaris*, *The Bird Hunter's Club*, and *20 Summers of Blood Sport*. My sincerest thanks to Bill, Tyler, Scott, Dodd, Jim, Johnny, and the rest of Team Realtree who've given me a platform and have been like extended family for most of my adult life. "Family,

Friends, and the Outdoors" is the Realtree company slogan, and it describes my own worldview just about perfectly.

Since 2020, I've also been a columnist and contributor to a couple print publications in the Outdoor Sportsman Group, including *Game & Fish* and, most notably, *Petersen's Hunting* (*PH*). I've enjoyed writing for these outlets immensely. "On Gates" originally appeared in *Game & Fish*. Both "Larry's Legacy" and "Elk Don't Gobble" (which was considered as the title story for the book) were written for *PH*. David Draper, who's mentioned a few times in this book, is the editor in chief of *PH*, and he invited me to write for them several years ago. I'm glad that he did.

"Shagbarks," "Joe's Pheasant," "A Date with Some Deer Piss," "Paid to Fish," and "The Thrash-Metal Turkey" are all original stories that I wrote for this book. All of the other stories were written in some form or another for *Field & Stream*, though several of them were heavily revised for this book. A magazine writer is usually limited by space, and so it was a joy to be able to tell these stories in full, as I've always wanted to tell them. When it comes to telling hunting and fishing stories, there's simply no place like *Field & Stream*. Brilliant editors like Dave Hurteau and Colin Kearns make it so. I owe thanks to both of those guys, along with the rest of the *Field & Stream* staff.

I want to thank my dad, who showed me what a shagbark hickory looks like and how to shoot a bow and a shotgun and how to call turkeys, and my mom, who didn't hunt or fish much herself but who would always drop me off at the bow shop on a Saturday or make sure I had a ride home from the Bass Hole after dark and who once helped me drag out a big 8-point buck while she was still in her nightgown.

And, finally, thanks to Michelle and Anse, my joy and my pride, respectively. I could stop hunting and fishing tomorrow and still have good stories to tell as long as both of you are by my side.

But for now, let's all keep hunting and fishing.

www.ingramcontent.com/pod-product-compliance
Ingram Content Group UK Ltd.
Pitfield, Milton Keynes, MK11 3LW, UK
UKHW040948220426
53221PUK00028B/61